Models of the Mind

Models

of the

Mind

a psychoanalytic theory

John E. Gedo
and
Arnold Goldberg

The University of Chicago Press
Chicago and London

JOHN E. GEDO is clinical professor of psychiatry at the Abraham Lincoln School of Medicine, the University of Illinois. He is also a training and supervisory analyst at the Chicago Institute for Psychoanalysis.

ARNOLD GOLDBERG is an attending psychiatrist at Michael Reese Hospital, Chicago. He is also a clinical associate professor of psychiatry at the Pritzker School of Medicine, the University of Chicago, and a training and supervisory analyst at the Chicago Institute for Psychoanalysis.

The University of Chicago Press, Chicago 60637
The University of Chicago Press, Ltd., London
© 1973 by The University of Chicago
All rights reserved. Published 1973
Printed in the United States of America
International Standard Book Number: 0–226–28484–0
Library of Congress Catalog Card Number: 73–77132

Contents

v

Foreword

I consider an invitation to write a foreword for this scholarly and definitive book an honor, especially since a systematic conceptualization of psychoanalytic theory is long overdue. Sigmund Freud alone created the basic theories and methods of psychoanalysis over a period of four decades. During his lifetime he abandoned, revised, and returned to many of his theories, as he personally increased his own understanding of mentation. But there was no repudiation of prior concepts, no public announcement of changed theories or models, and no specification of hypotheses. "The old and abandoned are mixed with the new which in some places is only implied" (Grinker 1968). The result was chaos. Countless papers were written about partial theories and their applications, with persistent semantic confusion.

Followers of Freud in psychoanalytic training institutes usually taught the historical development of theories, not their integration. They thereby weakened the usefulness of the theories and perpetuated so-called classical psychoanalysis, whose fragmentation could not be concealed by quotations from Freud and the use of a highly specialized language.

As a result, criticisms from scholars within and outside the psychoanalytic field mounted over the last two decades. These criticisms were repudiated by attributing "resistance" and lack of understanding to behavioral scientists, whose serious attempts at understanding were frustrated by the very inconsistency they criticized. These scientists could not grasp the whole and its internal structure, its relationship to external parameters, the absence of specific hypotheses, and the lack of empirical data, which Freud ceased to present in 1920. They responded to the accusation of "resistance" by referring to the self-styled designation of psychoanalysis as a "movement," or as "our science," thereby excluding behavioral scientists, who sincerely sought understanding and utilization of psychoanalysis.

Now come the authors of this monograph who attempt to synthesize the component parts of psychoanalytic theory by way of general systems theory. Without using this latter term, Anna Freud attempted an integration of the theories of development from childhood to adolescence. That this is a task of great difficulty is admitted in my own attempt in 1966, which I introduced as follows: "The specific focus here will be on the comparison of Freudian metapsychology and general systems theory as they conceptualize symbolism. Both, however, are global theoretical abstractions covering a variety of subtheories at varying distances from empirical data, so that some choices must be made. For this purpose I have chosen, not arbitrarily, topological theory of psychoanalysis and transactional theory as they apply to symbolism. Certainly this is not the only possible comparison, but the *easiest*" (1969).

This difficulty, which the authors bravely attack, is compounded by the fact that Freud's original theories constituted an open system since the reflex arc concept implied psychic and environmental transactions. But with the development of the theory of a death instinct, the theoretical system snapped closed. It was only much later, with the development of a theory of structure (the so-called tripartite theory), the theory of autonomy, and the inclusion of the adaptive point of view, that the psychoanalytic metapsychology became an open system. This had immense importance for what I called "open-system" psychiatry (1966).

Another among other problems the authors have solved in part is that resulting from the use of two unfortunate terms. One is "instinct," which should have been replaced by the less reductionistic "drives." Another is "metapsychology." This umbrella term, which covers the dynamic, economic, genetic, structural, and adaptive theories without integrating them, gives a false challenge which psychoanalytic writers feel compelled to meet and a false sense of certainty when met. As the authors indicate, the most supraordinate theory has not included a control or regulatory process which is not some vague metapsychology but is the self-system (Grinker 1957).

In attempting to use a general systems theory, one needs to define its components. Ten of these are itemized in the introduction to my *Toward a Unified Theory of Human Behavior* (1967). Jurgen Ruesch in the epilogue to the same book warns: "The output of any model has to be coded in terms that can be checked against the ongoing original events or against other scientific models. If the results coincide, the prediction or reconstruction of events becomes possible. If they do not coincide, the whole procedure has to be repeated with modification." This the authors acknowledge by their discussions.

In chapters 2 to 6 the authors recapitulate the development of psychoanalytic theory from the reflex, the topographic, the tripartite or structural, and the adaptive points of view and indicate that the theory of the self is still a dim outline toward which we are moving. Obviously not all of the details of psychoanalytic theory are suitable for their review, but the most substantial chunks are utilized and the others are disregarded. These early chapters are interesting because they consider Freud's own evolution by a systems approach. Here it becomes apparent that, as in all nature, continuities are not real but constitute human attempts to impose on the universe a certainty that does not exist in our real world of discontinuities.

This means that there is no one model of the mind. There is need and room for many. But for each model it is necessary that the position of the observer, the tools he uses, and what he is observing be specified. How, then, are these models connected? We have heard much of bridging concepts and language, for which we await passively, as for the arrival of the Messiah. The authors have chosen a developmental model for which they utilize five phases in transition whose heuristic value will have to be tested. This almost automatically forces them into a hierarchical system about which there is some scientific argument (chapter 7).

In chapters 8 to 10 the authors select Freud's own cases of the Rat Man, the Wolf Man, and the Schreber Case for reinterpretation according to their model, and, in my opinion, do this successfully.

Next is a chapter on nosology and implications for treatment. The type of the therapeutic problem is not specified by our current nosology but indicates where in the developmental series the patient is stuck or where he has regressed in the face of unresolvable conflict or external stress. Here the authors rely on a continuity pattern of health and illness which, I believe, is necessary because of the lack of the sharp jump-states in maturation. The implications for treatment are dependent on the phases of development and the sets of behaviors. There is no one treatment for all mentally ill, and many conditions require nonanalytic methods. Thus, many analysts should finally admit that "pacification, unification, optimal disillusion and interpretation" should be used when appropriate; at least they are guidelines to the beginning of therapy.

The last chapter has implications for theory, in that models are applied in a line of vertical maturation. This assumes importance for the behavioral scientist whose extrapsychoanalytic research may key into any point (a model or a stage of maturity) using his own concepts, hypotheses, tools, and criteria of validity. He then participates in a well-defined area, not in an amorphous jungle, and he can thus make systematic observations of specific phenomena. His position can be defined and what he observes can be focal. Thus, psychoanalysis as an open system becomes a part of the total scientific system at long last.

In 1957 I wrote: "There is a great need for psychoanalysis to become an open system with freer exchange through its boundaries. Progressive evolution does not occur in isolation but only through partial separation (specialization) to concentrate the genetic pool (conceptual formation) and by transactions with other groups to add gene symbols (communication) and to test them through natural selection (scientific method). This I hope will be the future course of psychoanalysis" (1958). To this end the authors have made a notable contribution.

One further point in gratitude to the authors. They not only indicate clearly the parts of their system-models but also how they are controlled, regulated, and organized around so-called "principles"—an understanding which is absolutely necessary, although often absent, in systems theory.

Finally, I advise the reader to peruse chapters 1 and 12 and to look at figures 1 to 10 before plunging into the book. It will make for better understanding of what I believe is a brilliant, scholarly, and necessary exposition of a most difficult subject.

Roy R. Grinker, Sr.

Acknowledgments

Some years ago, at an informal gathering, one of the authors asked the late Robert Waelder to discuss the most important developments in psychoanalysis in the last thirty-odd years. His answer was a characteristic one-liner, "Have there been any?"

This book is an effort to articulate the conviction that the clinical theory of psychoanalysis *has* made significant progress since the death of Freud, as it did in his lifetime. That this conviction, after much trial and error, is to be presented in this form to readers has been the result of help received from many quarters.

Dr. Roy R. Grinker, Sr., Director of the Psychiatric and Psychosomatic Institute of Michael Reese Hospital and Professor of Psychiatry, Pritzker School of Medicine of the University of Chicago, and Dr. Melvin Sabshin, Professor and Chairman, Department of Psychiatry, Abraham Lincoln School of Medicine, University of Illinois, both allowed us to devote time spent at these institutions to this pursuit.

Man, even scientific man, does not live by bread alone. We found the support necessary for our initiative from our former teacher of psychoanalytic theory at the Chicago Institute for Psychoanalysis, Dr. Heinz Kohut. He not only encouraged us to carry out our project but also suggested the specific focus of our study.

Each of these men has read several of the many drafts of this book and has given us essential feedback and valued criticism.

Similar help was graciously extended by so large a number of colleagues and friends that we finally became alarmed about having used up such a major segment of our potential readership. It is patently impossible to name everyone to whom we owe thanks for the thankless task of serving as our rehearsal audience. Nonetheless, there are a few individuals whose generous responses compel some special mention. Dr. Grinker's Foreword will give our readers some idea of the importance of the encouragement we have received from him. The most forceful testimony about the clinical usefulness of our approach came from Dr. M. Robert Gardner of Cambridge. Finally, we must express our special indebtedness to our last reader, Dr. Estelle Shane of Los Angeles, whose numerous suggestions have helped very appreciably with the readability of our complex subject matter.

The difficulties of collaborative authorship are nowhere more apparent than at the juncture we have reached here: how to express jointly our individual feelings toward those whose personal support provided the emotional matrix within which we were able to attempt creative work. Perhaps we can escape from this dilemma by relying, once again, on the capacity of these cherished persons to understand what they have meant to us without being told.

Acknowledgment is made to the following persons and publishers for permission to quote from the sources indicated: Carl P. Adatto—Carl P. Adatto, "Ego Reintegration Observed in Analysis in Late Adolescence," *International Journal of Psychoanalysis* 39. Aldine-Atherton, Inc.—H. Kohut and P. Seitz, "Concepts and Theories of Psycho-analysis," in *Concepts of Personality*, edited by J. Wepman and R. Heine. Balliere, Tindall, Ltd.—George Zavitzianos, "Problems of Technique in the Analysis of a Juvenile Delinquent," *International Journal of Psychoanalysis* 48, idem, "Fetishism and Exhibitionism in the Female and Their Relationship to Psychopathy and Kleptomania," *International Journal of Psycho-analysis* 52. Basic Books, Inc.—Sigmund Freud, *The Origins of Psychoanalysis,* edited by Anna Freud and Ernest Kris, translated by Eric Mosbacher and James

Strachey; *Collected Papers of Sigmund Freud,* edited by Ernest Jones, translated by Joan Riviere, Alix and James Strachey; Sigmund Freud, *The Interpretation of Dreams,* translated and edited by James Strachey; Sandor Ferenczi, *Sex in Psychoanalysis*; Ernest Jones, *The Life and Work of Sigmund Freud,* vol. 2. William Dawson and Sons—D. P. Schreber, *Memoirs of My Nervous Illness,* edited by Ida MacAlpine and Richard Hunter. Mrs. Robert Fliess—Robert Fliess, editor, *The Psychoanalytic Reader.* Sigmund Freud Copyrights Ltd., The Institute of Psychoanalysis, and the Hogarth Press Ltd.—*Standard Edition of the Complete Psychological Works of Sigmund ⁶Freud,* revised and edited by James Strachey. Harvard University Press—Suzanne Langer, *Philosophy in a New Key.* W. W. Norton Co.—Erik Erikson, *Young Man Luther.* International Universities Press, Inc.— Anna Freud, *The Ego and Mechanisms of Defence*; Anna Freud, *Normality and Pathology in Childhood*; D. Rapaport, *The Structure of Psychoanalytic Theory*; E. Glover, *On the Early Development of the Mind*; P. Greenacre, *Emotional Growth*; Hartmann, Kris, and Loewenstein, *Papers on Psychoanalytical Psychology*; A. Modell, *Object Love and Reality*; H. Nagera, *Psychoanalytic Study of the Child* XIX; H. Kohut, *Journal of the American Psychoanalytic Association* XIV.

I Introduction and Historical Review

1 The Problem: Current Clinical Theory in Psychoanalysis

Scientific theories are devised in order to gather together what has been learned, to give coherence to scientific findings. As such, they can never be considered final versions of truth; they can at best approximate validity. Some theories classify or categorize data to make predictions or to explain gaps in information. In contrast to such theories which grow out of the observational data, there are "hypothetico-deductive" propositions, theories which take a leap of the imagination away from the observables in order to postulate their causation. In this book, such theories which concern why things happen will not be considered; instead we will devote ourselves entirely to those theories which serve to *categorize* the clinical data collected through the psychoanalytic method.

Theories are useful only so long as they provide the most fruitful explanation of observations and must be discarded or modified when they cease to serve this function. Although psychoanalytic theory has been formulated as a framework of explanation for the clinical material collected during the psychoanalytic process, there has been some difficulty in fitting theory promptly to newly discovered facts. An outstanding example of this lag is in conceptualizing of mental function as a whole, as noted by Rapaport in 1951, when he pointed out that none of the psychoanalytic models of the mind satisfactorily portray every aspect of function represented by psychoanalytic data.

One common method of communicating a concept has been the construction of a model. A model is an ad hoc construction designed to make easier the understanding of complex, abstract theoretical propositions through the use of more easily encompassable pictorial or verbal analogies. Suzanne Langer has described models as follows:

A model always illustrates a principle of construction or operation, it is a symbolic projection of its object which need not resemble it in appearance at all but must permit one to match the factors of the model with respective factors of the object, according to some convention. The convention governs the selectiveness of the model; to all items in the selected class the model is equally true, to the limit of its accuracy, that is to the limit of the formal simplification imposed by the symbolic translation ([1962], p. 59).

Models of the mind are a special form of theoretical construction of traditional importance to psychoanalytic theory. They have been used as explanatory maps for analytic data. Those models of the mind most frequently utilized in psychoanalytic theory are those which successfully represent an up-to-date assessment of psychic functioning as seen in the observational setting of psychoanalysis in a relatively broad range of clinical conditions. And despite the importance of such models, as Rapaport pointed out, no completely satisfactory model of the mind exists.

In the course of his writings, Freud developed a whole series of conceptualizations of psychic functioning and accordingly created various models of the mind. That is, he changed from one theory and the use of a corresponding model, to another theory and its model whenever prior concepts failed to explain newly observed data. However, the changeover from one set of concepts to another need not indicate to us that one *superseded* the other. We believe that Freud did not intend to dispense with older concepts as he proposed newer ones; rather, he correctly assumed that a given set of data might be understood most clearly by utilizing one particular frame of reference or model of the mind, whereas another set of data demanded a different set of concepts for its clarification. This principle of several concurrent and valid avenues for organizing the data of observation we shall call "theoretical complementarity." This principle operates so long as no internal contradictions arise among the various parts of the theory. However, it requires that the proper sphere for the utilization of each portion be stringently defined. An example from another field may show the general applicability of the principle: neither a theory that conceptualizes light as waves, nor one that conceptualizes it as a succession of small, moving particles does justice to all the observable phenomena; a complete theory of light must, for the time being, utilize both hypotheses. With increasing knowledge, it may eventually be possible to arrive at a unitary hypothesis under which all previous theories of light may be subsumed as special instances.

Psychoanalysts have long been familiar with the concept of multiple variables in psychic phenomena, although the concept has not always been given sufficient emphasis. The principle of overdetermination, especially as applied to the interpretation of dreams and neurotic symptoms, is a prime example of analytic insistence that there is no *one* answer to a psychological question. Since Waelder's exposition in 1936 of the principle of multiple functioning of the psychic apparatus, it has been acknowledged that the "final pathway" in behavior is a compromise that serves many masters or psychic agencies; no single motive or most important factor can ever be isolated. Working within the framework of the then prevalent tripartite model of the mind, Waelder proved that all psychic phenomena simultaneously serve ego, id, superego, and adaptation to reality, as well as the complex interrelationships of these agencies with one another. Thus Waelder introduced the idea of multiple *interrelationships*. These should, however, be distinguished from the idea of multiple *variables* that had been embodied in the previously mentioned principle of overdetermination. A variable is a single addition to or change in a set of factors forming a system. Interrelationships describe the effects of variables upon one another.

Failure to take this concept of multiple variables into account may result in one or another form of theoretical reductionism. Although in the examination of complex phenomena it may be convenient to focus on simpler bits for ease of understanding or communicating, it is an error to think that the simplified concept is identical with or equivalent to the complexity. In other words, we can never succeed in "reducing" the unwieldy to the more manageable. One unhappy result of such efforts at neatness is a tendency to neglect the subtleties of psychic organization.

In addition to this need to examine psychological phenomena in terms of multiple variables in interaction, another issue must be kept in mind. This is the fact that the use of various vantage points from which to observe data will lead to the collection of differing data. Psychoanalysts should be on familiar ground in this regard. In the clinical setting, the many simultaneous aspects of transference show that the existing analytic situation as well as the attitude of the analyst-observer influences the nature of the material he elicits and the way in which he experiences it. To underscore the experiential aspect, it may be agreed that identical communications are experienced differently by the analyst in the early, defensive phases of the transference and at the height of a transference neurosis. It might be said that the material is actually different in subtle and affective terms, which merely means that we have succeeded in comprehending better how the changing perspective of the observer changes the object of study.

There are thus two issues to consider in theory formation: that of multiple variables in interaction and that of multiple perspectives. These issues are usually handled in clinical practice by various subtle, intuitive shifts by the analyst as he concentrates on one or another aspect of the patient's material, as he examines various categories or configurations of information, and as he runs the gamut of self-experiences. These same issues are not so easily handled in developing the clinical theories of psychoanalysis or its metapsychology. It is here that a "systems approach" may be of value.

General systems theory is the study of an organization and its parts in interaction. Its basic thesis is that complex interrelationships of any content follow similar rules and processes (cf. von Bertalanffy 1968). That is, whether one studies plants, animals or man, there exist common rules and patterns for the study of these complex phenomena. A study of these rules and processes allows one to grasp the organization of subsystems into larger wholes, at times according to hierarchical arrangements.[1] This approach is of particular value because of its open-endedness: aspects previously left out of consideration may be incorporated into the hierarchy at a later time by finding their proper articulation with existing subsystems.

We have said that systems theory consists in the codification of the common rules and patterns characteristic for the interrelationships of any set of complex phenomena. One example of such a rule is the principle of equifinality: a given end-result in a complex set of interactions may be obtained from many different initial conditions by traversing many different pathways. In analytic practice, this principle may be seen in operation in regard to the problem of the correct interpretation. We know that different interpretations may be equally "correct" on the basis of their leading to similar results.

The most effective application of the principles of systems theory to psychoanalysis has been Anna Freud's utilization of the concept of lines of development (1965). This concept organizes psychoanalytic data in a unique manner, different from previous modes of psychoanalytic conceptualization (cf. Lustman 1967). The lines of development represent coexisting sequences of behavior rather than cross-sectional views of psychic functioning at any given time. Her work can therefore serve as a basis for our effort to show that different behaviors can be observed from different vantage points, that these behaviors can be understood using a variety of clinical theories or models of the mind, and that these concepts can be organized according to a hierarchical overall arrangement.

Anna Freud has demonstrated that many areas of functioning or lines of growth can be traced through a person's life history. Some of the most important lines of development outlined, such as object relations, include libidinal phases, defenses, and various adaptive patterns. Any area of individual personality that represents interaction among maturation, adaptation, and structuralization may be followed in this novel manner. Anna Freud notes that in normality there is a general correspondence among the various developmental lines in their overall progress; imbalance among points of progression along various lines, on the other hand, is an indication of developmental difficulty or psychopathology. A valid assessment of individual personality requires consideration of all relevant lines and their complicated interactions in a total configuration. It is therefore necessary to develop criteria about which lines of development will be relevant for the identification of the various psychopathological entities.

In the field of psychology as a whole, the most effective application of systems theory has been the work of Jean Piaget in the area of cognitive studies. He has outlined and elaborated stages of cognitive development which can be further differentiated into substages, and which, in their overall organization, form an epigenetic system. Piaget makes it clear that such a sequential development leads to and implies systems of autoregulation. His use of the concept of "assimilation," the integration of new structures into the existing ones without a break in the continuity of functioning, has relevance for psychoanalysis. The formation of new structures is set in motion by the need to adapt to new situations. We hope to demonstrate that the concept of epigenetic schemata, that is, the interaction of the organism with the environment in a sequence of specific phases, is the most useful theoretical conception of the development of human mental functioning.

Let us now turn to the second requirement of nonreductionistic theory, the capacity to account for variations in perspective. The methods of data collection utilized for theory building in psychoanalysis are principally observations made within the psychoanalytic treatment process and, in a more limited way, the direct observation of infants. These data are then organized by means of various constructs or models at increasing levels of abstraction and range all the way from the borders of biology to the philosophical statements of epistemology. This variety of theoretical tools is entirely appropriate, since various levels of function within a total system may operate in accord with different sets of laws. It is also perfectly proper to utilize a number of different models of psychic functioning, arranged in accord with a Jacksonian schema of hierarchies (cf. Rapaport 1950, 1951).

The dictionary definition of hierarchy is that of a system of levels according to which something is organized. Piaget states that hierarchical order occurs in every differentiation of an organization. The most general "form" found in a hierarchy is the inclusion of a part or substructure into one whole or total structure. According to Bertalanffy's description of an organism, there are many kinds of hierarchies within it. For our purposes, "hierarchy" will indicate connections of various subsystems into an overall organization with differing levels of regulation. The concept of levels in a hierarchy does not imply that any one level is of greater importance than any other but is mainly of significance in terms of the observer's grasp of the relationships among the subsystems. The series gastric cell-stomach-digestive system constitutes a hierarchical order; although the stomach is but a subsystem of the digestive apparatus, one cannot say that it is of more or less importance than the gastric cell.

It follows that the concept of hierarchy implies that the various models used for the proper organization and ordering of the data need not have equal status. Models may represent concepts at different levels of abstraction. This fact must not be misused, however, to make value judgments about the behaviors to which the models may be applied. A model is a tool, and one tool is no better than another, although in performing a specific task certain tools are more useful than others. For example, an ordering of clinical data at a level close to observation (in such a statement as "obsessive-compulsive neurotics struggle with control of affect") differs from one conceptualized on a more abstract basis ("obsessive-compulsive neurotics struggle with a harsh superego"). Both formulations are equally useful; one is no better than the other; each must be used at different times according to specific needs for organizing clinical data.

Similarly, all models of the mind are of equal importance, but, because they are applicable to different levels of the hierarchy, they are not comparably useful in organizing the understanding of a given problem. The various analytic models should therefore be arranged into a hierarchy, too, and the appropriate function of each one in explaining various subsystems or modes of psychic life should be delineated. Such a hierarchical arrangement of models, paralleling the hierarchy of modes of psychic functioning, will constitute a supraordinate model of the mind. This could then be used in whole or in part, on a flexible basis, as the situation demands. Unfortunately, such complexity is not easy to keep in mind, and there is always a strong temptation to abandon the richness of multiple points of view in favor of some simpler, unitary model. It is, of course, not illegitimate to order phenomena in their totality by means of any particular model, but to do so may unduly restrict appreciation of the manifold perspectives from which the data may be seen.

Waelder (1962) has arranged the propositions of psychoanalytic theory in hierarchical order, differentiating metapsychological propositions at the highest levels of abstraction, from the interpretations, generalizations, and clinical theories into which analytic observations may be organized at lower levels. Metapsychology consists of ad hoc, noninductive explanatory concepts which within themselves also differ in levels of abstraction. The very highest level of this hierarchy of propositions consists of the "points of view" of metapsychology. Rapaport and Gill (1959) enumerated these as the dynamic, economic, genetic, structural, and adaptive viewpoints. These five are considered by many to be the basic assumptions of psychoanalytic theory. In this view, all other propositions can and must be viewed simultaneously from these multiple perspectives. Thus, all psychoanalytic theories of mental functioning should embody each of these points of view.

Models of the mind are summarizing conventions which represent the clinical theory of psychoanalysis. The principles of their organization may follow some or all of the points of view of metapsychology. Thus a specific model may show the interaction of dynamic forces or it may represent structures, or both, and so on. A number of different models may be devised to represent a particular theory. Some readers do not find graphic representations (the "symbolic translations" of Suzanne Langer) to be clearer than the verbal statements of the theory they are intended to portray. This reaction merely shows that models of the mind are simply conveniences, useful to some but not to all. It is the theory they serve that is primary. In order to maintain this differentiation between models and theories, we shall consistently distinguish the "tripartite model," for example, from the "structural theory" to which it corresponds.

A number of recent efforts have been made to reconcile the various commonly used models in psychoanalytic theory (see Gill 1963, Arlow and Brenner 1964, Sandler and Joffe 1969). In our opinion, such attempts derive from the assumption that it is presently possible to construct a single model representing the totality of mental life. It should be noted, however, that none of the functions which develop autonomously or later gain autonomy have found representation in any model based on the clinical theories of psychoanalysis, all of which have been devised to explain mental conflicts. It is unwarranted to claim that certain autonomous functions, such as perception or cognition, are implied in the models; it would be just as legitimate to claim that these diagrams imply an intact digestive system. Should the issue of digestion, or perception, or cognition be introduced into clinical theory, the models would have to be revised to show these functions in some explicit manner.

Perhaps even more crucial than the neglect of autonomous functions in all existing models is the omission of the genetic point of view from them, in spite of its importance in the clinical theories they are designed to represent. Consequently, it may not be possible to devise one model which adequately portrays all of the crucial aspects of psychic life. It may be more feasible to construct models of the mind based on the principle that a different model may be most useful and theoretically valid for the study of each of the various phases of an individual's life history. Each of these models may represent only those aspects of mental life having the greatest importance for that specific phase of development. If these various incomplete and even imperfect models can be arranged in a sequence, reflecting the succession of developmental phases which they portray in their most crucial functional attributes, such a chronologically organized schema may permit the most convenient exposition of the gradual unfolding of mental life. It would, of course, constitute a major fallacy to assume that it is the successive models in the schema which develop or change from the earlier to the later ones, or that the last stage has *Anlagen* in all the others.

We are espousing the epigenetic concept of development as opposed to its alternative, the concept of preformation. Epigenesis views the formation of structure as the result of successive trans- actions between the organism and its environment; the outcome of each phase is understood to depend on the outcomes of all previous phases. Each new phase integrates the previous phases and has a new level of organization and regulation. A model to portray this new organization may therefore have to be based on entirely different principles for representation than were optimal for the previous levels of organization. As Hartmann and Loewen- stein have pointed out (1962), biology has now discarded the notion that the grown form of the organism is preformed from its earliest beginnings. They have also shown how tenaciously the concept of preformation has lingered on in psychoanalytic theory. However, an explicit epigenetic schema has been pro- posed by Erikson (1950). He has attempted to build a bridge between individual and social psychology through its formula- tion. In contrast, our work will focus exclusively on the psychol- ogy of the intrapsychic world, derived from psychoanalytic data.

We should like to underline the importance of the epigenetic view by means of a specific example, that of superego formation. The tripartite model, first proposed by Freud in *The Ego and the Id* (1923) to illustrate the structural theory, has been put for- ward most frequently as the model of the mind which might be used in place of all others. This model serves admirably to ex- plain a wide range of psychoanalytic observations in terms of conflicts among the agencies of the mind it postulates. One of these, the internalized agency of morality, is the superego. Be- cause the tripartite model assumes the existence of the superego as a functional unit of the mind, it is an optimal tool for the study of certain kinds of psychopathology, namely, disorders re- sulting from various faulty resolutions of the Oedipal phase of development, since the superego is formed as a consequence of the resolution of the Oedipus complex. If one has to consider data about mental functioning in persons in whom this developmental experience has not yet taken place, such as very young children or certain persons with atypical development, then the tripartite model is inadequate. The fully formed superego does not stem from a smaller predecessor; it is an entirely new psychic agency. To be sure, the regulatory functions of the superego are performed in other ways before its formation. Bicycles, automobiles, and airplanes are all modes of transportation; however, bicycles do not turn into autos, and cars do not grow wings to make them fly. Conversely, the precursors of airplanes were not more pedestrian modes of transport, but toys such as kites and balloons.

With regard to the superego, Hartmann and Loewenstein (1962) have expressed this same idea.

Genetic determinants of the superego have often been termed its forerunners, or forestages, or primordia. There is nothing to be said against any of these terminological distinctions, as long as one keeps in mind the differences between function and genesis . . . and as long as one sees these factors only as genetic determinants and not as part of the system superego. . . . It is very likely that a genetic tie leads from what Ferenczi called "sphincter morality" to the later superego; but the word "morality" is misleading in this context because it neglects the difference we have in mind . . . (p. 146).[2]

We feel that even the term "superego precursor" may lead one to slip back to the mistaken notion that this structure grows out of earlier, albeit smaller and less efficient, self-regulating agencies. The essential property of superego functioning, that of internal self-regulation, especially with regard to moral considerations, is simply absent before the formation of this new psychic agency at the time of the resolution of the Oedipus complex. Conforming behavior based on the fear of external consequences, such as punishment or the loss of love, precedes the acquisition of true morality. At even earlier stages, conduct may be regulated through primitive identifications. The mental structures upon which these types of behavior are based, for example, memories of the cautioning and prohibiting external figure of the father of the two-year-old, have to be represented in a model of the mind in some manner different from the three mental agencies shown in the tripartite model.

In any model of the mind the successive stages of development are artificially represented as discontinuities. In real life, discontinuity of function does not occur, and developmental stages unfold in a manner that allows for the assimilation of new structures. There are always regulating functions at work, for example; this is implicit in the concept of lines of development. At various phases within a given line, the function of behavior regulation is carried out by structural units of the mind which, at subsequent phases, may assume entirely different functions, only to be succeeded at the task of self-regulation by a new set of structures. Although the structural point of view is always essential for psychoanalysts' understanding, the tripartite model is truly applicable only within a limited range of the developmental line.

Such a definition of its range of optimal applicability is not a criticism of the usefulness of this model or of the theory of mental function which it represents. However, attempts to use the structural theory to clarify phenomena that lie outside of its optimal range have been labored and unsatisfactory. Such attempts lead to excessive reliance on descriptions of the absence or poverty of more mature structures, such as a diagnosis of "superego lacunae." It would be more helpful, instead, to focus on the functioning of those structures which are actually present. In the same example, this would involve clarification of the manner in which a delinquent's behavior is actually regulated. The problem extends, to be sure, to every misapplication of theory to data; witness how pained we are in the explication of certain problems, such as the negative therapeutic reaction, in terms of the topographic theory and model which utilize only the concepts of opposed unconscious and preconscious systems, without utilizing the superego.

To illustrate the principles of an epigenetic schema (to be discussed more fully in chapter 6), we should like to offer a diagrammatic version of one important line of personality development, that of the classical "situations of danger" (see Strachey 1953–, 20:81). These are typical situations that generate the affects of anxiety or fear at successive phases of development. The fact that a danger situation is "typical" for a given phase does not mean that it is the only one pertinent for it. Nor do danger situations disappear once they cease to be the typical one; they all persist throughout the life cycle. The earliest typical danger is that of traumatic overstimulation. Then, following the development of the capacity to differentiate a reliable object, the principal danger becomes the possibility of the loss of this need-satisfying object. This is gradually refined into fear of the loss of the object's love. There follows an era of function in which the typical danger is that of castration. After establishment of the superego, this is succeeded by the danger of intersystemic conflict between ego and superego, that is, of moral anxiety. The last stage, following consolidation of the repression barrier, is one in which realistic external threats constitute the typical danger.

This line of development may be represented diagrammatically through the use of a rectangular coordinate graph (see fig. 1).

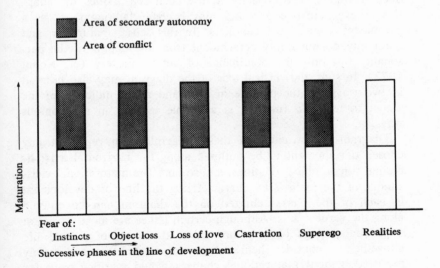

Fig. 1. Line of development of the typical situations of danger.

From left to right, the graph shows the unfolding or stepwise progression of increasingly complex psychological functions along its horizontal axis. Thus the horizontal axis has two simultaneous meanings: on the one hand, it represents the passage of time; on the other, if viewed in terms of one particular moment, it shows the various possibilities of the particular function which are available to the person. The vertical axis is intended to show transformations of the specific psychological configurations that enter mental life at successive periods, as they undergo their own maturation.[3] We use the "maturation" to designate the increasing autonomy each psychic function gains in time, that is, its relative freedom from regression under stress. Maturation, in this sense, is in keeping with the customary idea that growth is determined by constitutional givens; at the same time, we restrict our usage to instances in which this growth leads to secondary autonomy. Hartmann (1939) has designated this process as a "change of function." As an example, we might cite the gradual attenuation of castration fear that may enable a person to attain special sensitivity about the effects his aggressiveness may produce in others. The capacity to use such sensitivities for adaptive or even creative purposes may become "autonomous" as a permanent asset of the character. In this sense, maturation and autonomy do not imply detachment from the depths of the personality but only the dominance of active mastery (cf. Kohut 1972). In sum, the vertical axis of the diagram may also be read in two ways: as the passage of time and as an indicator of the extent to which a function is available for use in autonomous ways.

Diagrams constructed on these principles can represent any chosen development to be outlined along the horizontal axis: libidinal stages, object relations, and so on.[4] The maturational vicissitudes of the main issue characterizing the line of development in each of the phases charted on the diagram can be entered along the vertical axis. Although certain issues are most crucial at a particular stage of life, they never drop out of mental life altogether; to consider them at later stages as if they had merely persisted without maturational changes would sacrifice truth for the sake of simplicity. As for the most crucial matter, that of the choice of lines of development to be entered on the diagram, it is necessary to determine which issues of mental life are most relevant for the differentiation of various types of mental functioning, normal and pathological.

The epigenetic approach is by no means new in psychoanalysis. Freud (1905d) constructed an epigenetic theory of the libido, doubtless influenced by Hughlings Jackson's emphasis on the stepwise developmental progression of neurological structures and on the persistence of earlier organizations within the later ones. Freud stressed that each stage of the libido, though it was followed by another, continued to persist throughout life. He did not feel that the derivatives of infantile component drives are necessarily indicative of fixations at the various primitive developmental levels. Moreover, he did not regard regressions to points of fixation as automatic indicators of pathology.

Clinical experience suggests that various stages of the libido should also be conceptualized as having their own maturation. Each component of the libido—orality, anality, and so on—has its own fate throughout life. It is necessary to differentiate adequate development along a specific maturational axis from pathological fixations. It must be spelled out explicitly that a depressed person with an oral fixation is quite different in his orality from a gourmet. One must do more than make reference to the general maturation of the ego in order to distinguish primitive from mature orality. In a discussion of orality, such a reference to maturation of the ego amounts to nothing more specific than a statement that the whole person is more mature. Detailed explanations are needed of those changes in function which, as a whole, add up to "ego development." We can define orality as an instinctual drive that undergoes changes from its original primitive state to more mature, "neutralized" forms; from archaic aims and objects to those more appropriate in later life; and from a stage of unintegrated discharge to one of increasingly complex synthesis within the totality of the personality.

These considerations apply to any developmental sequence of functions we may choose to examine: object relations, the situations of danger, the regulation of behavior, to mention a few. Epigenesis has been a constant theme in the ordering of psychoanalytic data by Freud and his successors. This was first made explicit by Ferenczi who coined the term "lines of development" to designate successive stages in the ontogeny of mental functions (1911, 1913). The concept has been used most extensively by Anna Freud (1965). It now needs to be applied to the problems of psychopathology and to the theory of therapeutics.

As we have already stated, epigenesis demonstrates the increasing complexity of mental life as the organism grows. The sequence of higher levels of organization resulting in new modes of autoregulation functions without overt discontinuity. Development is divided into stages arbitrarily, for didactic purposes; some of these stages are more clear-cut than others. The use of a clinical theory, of a diagram, or of a model applicable to one of these stages might suggest a discontinuity which has no basis in reality. We shall attempt to demonstrate that different theories and their models illuminate the data of various discrete developmental phases. Freud's topographic approach of 1900 seems adequate for the elucidation of "successful" dreams, jokes, parapraxes, and isolated neurotic symptoms. The tripartite model of *The Ego and the Id* (1923) best explains phenomena produced by unconscious ego and superego conflicts. It is therefore most useful for the understanding of character disorders, traumatic dreams, and certain superego problems. Attempts to explain psychoses, narcissistic personality disorders, and other issues of the primitive psyche through the use of either of these models must utilize explanations which stress deficiencies or absence of structure, such as "weakness of the ego" or "defectiveness of the repression barrier." The lack of age-appropriate structuralization is an important finding, but it does not explain how the mind is actually operating. As an analogy for the misuse of one of these theories, we offer the formulation that a crawling baby is suffering from an absence of the capacity to walk. Although it has not reached the level of muscular development required for walking, the crawler is not well described by statements about its incapacity to walk. Crawling may be followed by walking, but the two processes are truly separate activities.

Thus far, no satisfactory set of concepts has been proposed for the study of the psyche before its differentiation into id-ego-superego. About this gap in analytic theory, Modell has said:

The area of clinical experience that awaits better conceptualization is that of disturbed human object relationships. What is now needed is a model that would better conceptualize the ego's [self's] relationship to the environment and would encompass progressive and regressive alterations in object relations (1968, p. 125).

A model of this kind could be based on the numerous psychoanalytic findings of the differentiation of the self from objects. These developmental data are often less than adequately clear, however, when they are presented in the form and terminology of the structural theory and the tripartite model. One task of this study will be to present an alternative method of organizing these data (see especially chapter 5).

The plan of this work can be listed as follows.

1. To describe the principal, relevant psychoanalytic theories and models of the mind in order to define their ranges of optimal use.

2. To delineate further concepts implicit in accepted psychoanalytic theory and essential for the study of the primitive psyche.

3. To select and describe those lines of development needed for making the most important nosological distinctions in a psychoanalytically meaningful manner.

4. To correlate these lines of development into an overall hierarchical model of the manner in which all the hitherto described subsystems are interrelated.

5. To subject the entire system to some tests of clinical applicability.

6. To outline certain clinical and theoretical implications which follow from the establishment of this model of mental function.

Throughout this monograph, clinical data will be presented in order to illustrate the theoretical discussion. We cannot make an effort to show the inductive reasoning that led to the formation of particular psychoanalytic theories on the basis of these or similar clinical observations. We shall content ourselves with the more modest task of trying to demonstrate how much of the material of a given case history is illuminated by being organized in accord with the theory under consideration—and how much of it cannot be conceptualized meaningfully by utilizing that theory. This will amount to a test of how far each theory and its corresponding model will go in facilitating the reduction and ordering of clinical data.

The major methodological problem presented by this task is that of the reliability of the clinical observations to be utilized for the test.[5] This problem is of the greatest magnitude in relation to data collected by the investigator in his own clinical practice. The elaborate safeguards necessary to eliminate the distorting effects of our unconscious biases are beyond our capacity to arrange. We shall attempt to sidestep this problem by dealing, insofar as this will be possible, with a familiar body of observations within the public domain: the published clinical evidence of Sigmund Freud. We shall supplement this set of data with other published case material only where appropriate examples do not occur in Freud's work. Needless to say, there will be no effort to be comprehensive in presenting Freud's clinical evidence. We shall confine our attention to case reports which provide sufficient detail for our purposes.[6]

Although the reliability issue is not eliminated altogether by selecting the case histories of respected authorities for examination, it is reduced to the task of reflecting the familiar data in a reliable manner. Our presentations will assume that the reader has seen the original case reports; these should be consulted again for optimal understanding of our discussion as well as for assessing the accuracy and representativeness of our versions.

We are following a respected psychoanalytic tradition in using the "classical" case histories to test various theories of mental function and models of the mind. Freud himself had returned to the case of Little Hans in 1926 to try out the tripartite model (1926 [1925], pp. 101–4, 124–26), and Anna Freud did so to illustrate her work on the defenses (1936, pp. 73–88). In other words, whatever shortcomings Freud's case histories may suffer from on the score of their reliability, these deficiencies remain constant no matter which conceptual tools are being utilized. Consequently, for purposes of testing these tools, the reliability issue may be overlooked.

2 Freud's Clinical Theory of 1900: The Topographic Model

As we stated in the previous chapter, a review is in order of the principal theoretical tools constructed by Freud which have continued in use to the present day. We undertake this historical survey not only to include a reliable summary description of each model of the mind and of its significance, but also to demonstrate that each model corresponds to a different clinical theory. To put this in another way, at various times Freud studied different subject matters, separate clinical phenomena, each calling for separate theoretical explanations. For each occasion he developed appropriate theories and, for didactic purposes, embodied these in various models. Thus each of his principal models attempts to represent a different facet of mental functioning, so that these schemata are not interchangeable. Because they were chosen on an ad hoc basis to meet differing didactic needs, no single guiding principle runs through these varied concepts, and there is no simple way of organizing the relationships among them. Our task will be to suggest a way in which these relationships can be organized.

THE TOPOGRAPHIC MODEL

Freud constructed an explicit model of the mental apparatus for the first time in *The Interpretation of Dreams* (1900); his earlier theoretical efforts to explain psychic functioning did not include actual graphic models. The initial model was thus proposed in the context of describing and explaining the psychology of dream processes (1900a, chap. 7).

Freud's starting point was the ubiquitous phenomenon of the forgetting of dreams which indicated to him a strengthening of an endopsychic censorship when the dreamer awakes. It is the reduction of the power of the censorship during the sleeping state that makes the formation of dreams possible, and even in the manifest dream Freud detected the activity of the censorship in the form of displacements, condensations, and the like. These aspects of the dream work make the latent meaning of the dream unintelligible, and therefore permit the entry of the manifest dream into consciousness. Freud postulated that similar compromises were at work in the formation of psychoneurotic symptoms.

The dream work usually transforms latent dream thoughts into visual or auditory percepts through which an unacceptable wish is represented as fulfilled. In order to explain this phenomenon, Freud relied on a statement by Fechner to the effect that "the scene of action of dreams is different from waking ideational life." He wrote to Fliess, "It has been left to me to draw the first crude map of it" (1950 [1892–99], letter 83). The metaphor of the map indicates that Freud's first model of the mind was designed to illustrate the idea of "psychical locality." It is for this reason that it has come to be called a "topographic" model (see fig. 2).

Freud was most careful to differentiate his model from the realities it was intended to clarify:

Analogies of this kind are only intended to assist us in our attempt to make the complications of mental functioning intelligible. . . . We are justified, in my view, in giving free rein to our speculations so long as we retain the coolness of our judgment and do not mistake the scaffolding for the building (1900a, p. 536).

Accordingly, Freud made an analogy between the mental apparatus and a compound optical instrument, the components of which he named "systems" or "agencies."[1] In a preliminary version of the model, the temporal sequence of psychic processes was shown by means of spatial ordering between a sensory end of the apparatus and a motor one. This is a representation of the conception that motor activity follows upon perception after some kind of intrapsychic processing of the percepts.

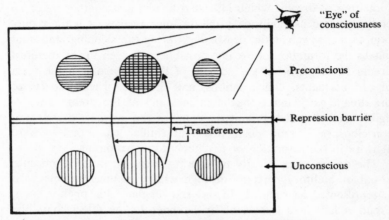

Fig. 2. The Topographic Model (from Kohut and Seitz 1963).

The perceptual system had already been differentiated from other intrapsychic processes by Breuer (Breuer and Freud 1895). He had pointed out that the perceptual system must be organized in a manner permitting restoration to a resting state as rapidly as possible. In contrast, the memory systems must be capable of undergoing permanent modification. Therefore, in his spatial model, Freud placed the memory systems between the perceptual and the motor ones.[2] In accord with the multiple ways in which memories may be associated, such as simultaneity in time or relations of similarity, several mnemic systems were introduced into the diagram.

Freud then attempted to organize the evidence obtained from the study of dreams by means of this schema:

we were only able to explain the formation of dreams by venturing upon the hypothesis of there being two psychical agencies, one of which submitted the activity of the other to a criticism which involved its exclusion from consciousness. The critical agency, we concluded, stands in a closer relation to consciousness than the agency criticized: it stands like a screen between the latter and consciousness. Further, we found reasons for identifying the critical agency with the agency which directs our waking life and determines our voluntary, conscious actions. If . . . we replace these agencies by systems, our last conclusion must lead us to locate the critical system at the motor end of the apparatus (p. 540).

Stated in these terms, the model distinguishes a system "unconscious" from a system "preconscious" (see fig. 2). Freud gave these the designations *Ucs.* and *Pcs.*

Consciousness was at this time conceptualized by Freud as "a sense organ for the apprehension of psychical qualities." He assumed that it could receive excitations from the perceptual system on the one hand, and from within the psychic apparatus itself on the other. He thought, however, that the only processes which possessed psychical qualities initially were those of energy transpositions, experienced either as pleasure or as unpleasure. With psychic development, consciousness adds to its initial capacity to register only perceptions of pleasure and unpleasure and becomes a sense organ for a larger portion of intrapsychic processes. This change occurs when preconscious processes become linked with the mnemic system of linguistic symbols, which processes thereby acquire perceptual qualities.

Subsequent to this change, the contents of the *Pcs.*, which are predominantly attached to word presentations, are capable of entering consciousness whenever they receive sufficient attention cathexis. The contents of the *Ucs.* never have direct access to consciousness; in order to be perceived, they must first pass through the *Pcs.*, undergoing modification in the process. In other words, the unconscious dream wish may enter consciousness only following suitable alterations resulting from its passage through the preconscious. It is these alterations that Freud defined as the dream work. Most often, dream work consists in the amalgamation of the infantile wish with a preconscious day residue. The outcome is experienced in an archaic manner, usually as a visual hallucination, which results from the regression of the formal aspects of thinking during sleep. Although hallucinations may occur in the waking state on the basis of the same intrapsychic processes, more often regressive states in waking life do not involve the formal aspects of thinking, so that they generally produce different results. Nevertheless, these alternative phenomena also involve the "transference" of *Ucs.* material onto *Pcs.* contents.

Freud made it quite clear that the model of mental function he had constructed was applicable only to conditions in adults. He stated this in the course of his discussion of the conclusion that the dream wish must be an infantile one:

In the case of adults it originates in the *Ucs.*, in the case of children, where there is as yet no division or censorship between the *Pcs.* and *Ucs.*; or where that division is only gradually being set up, it is an unfulfilled, unrepressed wish from waking life (p. 553).

In other words, before the secure establishment of the two separate systems of mental functioning, one cannot properly speak of "transference" phenomena. Consequently, the concepts of topographic theory are not applicable to infantile organization.[1]

However, the fact was ignored that Freud had been explicit in limiting the range of applicability of the topographic model, even though he continued to add instances of these limits to later editions of *The Interpretation of Dreams*. In certain addenda of 1919, for instance, he took up the matter of anxiety dreams and "punishment" dreams. He demonstrated that the wishes fulfilled in dreams which might be termed "unsuccessful" do not belong to the repressed but to the "the ego," designated at this time as the critical agency that determines voluntary behavior. Thus, in violation of the topographical model, the criterion of accessibility to consciousness was abandoned as the cardinal explanatory principle in anxiety and punishment dreams. In effect, Freud was defining another boundary of the applicability of the topographic model: not only is it unserviceable in the case of children and certain personality types in adults which will be specified in later chapters; it is also less than satisfactory in explaining unsuccessful dreams. Freud added that the issues involved in anxiety and punishment dreams could not be clarified without going beyond the boundaries of dream psychology. These necessary revisions of his theoretical views were not to be made until 1923, in *The Ego and the Id*.[2]

In 1900 Freud had also been obliged to adduce evidence from the study of the neuroses to complete his conceptualization of topographic theory:

We learn from [this study] that an unconscious idea is as such quite incapable of entering the preconscious and that it can only exercise any effect there by establishing a connection with an idea which already belongs to the preconscious, by transferring its intensity on to it and by getting itself "covered" by it. Here we have the fact of "transference" . . . The preconscious idea, which thus acquires an undeserved degree of intensity, may either be left unaltered by the transference, or it may have a modification forced upon it, derived from the content of the idea which effects the transference (pp. 562–63).

In dream formation the preconscious contents utilized in this manner are the day residues: memories of indifferent percepts, which "have least to fear from the censorship."

In waking life, "the censorship between the *Ucs.* and the *Pcs.* . . . deserves to be recognized and respected as the watchman of our mental health." At this time Freud thought that with failure of the censorship a psychosis would result. From this view we may infer that Freud did not regard the topographic model as applicable to the phenomena of the psychoses. Its usefulness ends with the indication that the demarcation between the two mental systems breaks down in some manner before the psychotic phenomenology can occur. We do not mean to imply that the limitations of the topographic theory render it erroneous, but despite its usefulness the topographic model leaves large areas of mental life unaccounted for; psychosis is just one of these omissions.[3]

Primary processes operate in accordance with the "unpleasure principle."[4] Whenever behavior is governed by them, the person will not perceive anything unpleasant. This automatic avoidance of unpleasure is the prototype of repression. Secondary process thinking is based on the acquisition of the capacity to cathect even unpleasurable memories. This achievement is made possible by the development of the capacity to inhibit the emergence of the unpleasure caused by the unpleasant memory. Eventually, the affect generated by thought activity must be reduced to the minimum intensity required to act as a signal. Repression proper occurs whenever *Pcs.* contents to which *Ucs.* intensities have been transferred are "left to themselves." This means that consciousness has been turned away from them under the sway of the unpleasure principle. Therefore the occurrence of repression proper presupposes the secure differentiation between the two psychic systems.

Moreover, the topographic model permitted Freud to explain disturbances in mental functioning on a "dynamic" basis, that is, through the concept of the strengthening and weakening of the various components in the interplay of forces (cf. 1900a, p. 608). In addition to successful dreams and psychoneurotic symptoms, the mental products he examined by means of this model were parapraxes and jokes. The former were discussed in detail in *The Psychopathology of Everyday Life* (1901) and the latter in *Jokes and Their Relation to the Unconscious* (1905c).

However, Freud was careful to end *The Interpretation of Dreams* with a warning about the deficiencies of the topographic model. His concluding section stresses the economic viewpoint which had found no graphic representation therein. The concept of energic cathexes replaced the spatial metaphors of the topographic model in this final discussion.

A CLINICAL ILLUSTRATION OF THE USE OF TOPOGRAPHIC CONCEPTS

Among Freud's major case histories, the one that comes closest to illustrating topographic concepts without leaving too many loose ends is the 1909 report on "a case of obsessional neurosis," commonly referred to as the Rat Man (cf. Zetzel 1966).[5] The patient was a twenty-nine-year-old lawyer who had suffered from obsessional symptoms since early childhood. For over four years he had had intense fears of harming either his father or a woman he admired; he also had impulses to cut his own throat. The struggle against his obsessions was increasingly impoverishing his professional and personal life. His difficulties had come to a head during army maneuvers the summer prior to seeking treatment in 1907. He became obsessed with the fantasy that his father and beloved lady would be subjected to a torture he had heard of which involved rats eating their way into the victim's anus. This idea was warded off by means of magical formulas made up of words or gestures which eventuated in ceremonials of repetitive doing and undoing.

The patient's earliest memories related to the death of an older sister who had been very close to him, and to an attack of rage against his father. These were events from the fourth or fifth year of his life. He recalled having intense sexual curiosity around the same ages. By the age of six he had developed the feeling that his voyeuristic wishes would kill his father. In order to prevent his father's demise, he had to set up compulsive rituals to undo the effects of his scoptophilic wishes. Similar obsessions recurred when, at the age of twenty, he fell in love with his cousin. Remarkably, these fears persisted in spite of the fact that his father actually died when the patient was twenty-one. The exacerbation of the obsessions that preceded the analysis had followed rejection by his cousin and the emergence of a plan to marry another woman.

As Jones (1955) has noted, the analysis lasted only eleven months but the result was brilliant. A number of significant additions to clinical theory were presented on the basis of the data (cf. Jones 1955, pp. 262–68). In this account, however, we will confine our attention to the manner in which clinical theory and clinical data interact. It is of interest to review how much complex phenomenology Freud was able to explain on the basis of topographic concepts alone. He was able to show how the repressed found its way into the magical formulas that had been set up for the purpose of warding it off; in other words, he demonstrated that the defensive struggle concerning the symptomatic idea takes place at the repression barrier. One brief example may illustrate this:

During his religious period he had made up prayers for himself which took up more and more time . . . the reason being that something always inserted itself into the simple phrases and turned them into their opposite. E.g., "May God—not—protect him". . . . He had suddenly

given all this up eighteen months ago; i.e., he had made up a word out of the initials of some of his prayers . . . (1909d, p. 260).
It was Glejisamen:—
gl = *glückliche*, i.e., may L. [Lorenz] be happy; also, [may] all [be happy].
e = (meaning forgotten)
j = *Jetzt und immer* [now and ever]
i = (present faintly beside the j)
s = (meaning forgotten)
It is easy to see that this word is made up of

$$\overset{\frown}{\text{GISELA}}$$
$$\text{S AMEN}$$

and that he united his "*Samen*" [semen] with the body of his beloved . . . sometimes the formula had secondarily taken the shape of gisela-men (ibid., p. 280).[6]

Freud explained the neurosis as a whole on the basis of repression of Oedipal hatred of the father as well as of the rejecting woman, followed by a dual regression: that of the libido from phallic aims to anal sadistic ones, and that of action to the sphere of erotized thought. Freud was not completely satisfied with these explanations, and he ended the case history with a delimitation of what he had left unexplored:

What is characteristic of this neurosis . . . is not . . . to be found in instinctual life but in the psychological field. I cannot take leave of my patient without putting on paper my impression that he had, as it were, disintegrated into three personalities: into one unconscious personality, that is to say, and into two preconscious ones between which his consciousness could oscillate. His unconscious comprised those of his impulses which had been suppressed at an early age and which might be described as passionate and evil impulses. In his normal state he was kind, cheerful, sensible—an enlightened and superior kind of person—while in his third psychological organization he paid homage to superstition and asceticism. . . . This second preconscious personality comprised chiefly the reaction-formations against his repressed wishes . . . (pp. 248–49).

This remarkable passage demonstrates that in 1909 Freud was already aware of the inadequacies of the topographic model for clarifying the intrapsychic conflicts determining the character structure of neurotic personalities. He was for the first time looking at behavior from the point of view of three sets of stable functional characteristics in conflict with one another. His formulations were confined to clinical generalizations,[7] the building blocks upon which his future metapsychological constructs would have to be based (cf. Gedo et al. 1964). Except for the fact that he did not describe the unconscious aspects of the ego and superego, Freud had already divided the Rat Man's personality in the manner he was to portray through the tripartite model.

During the period from 1909, when the Rat Man was described, and 1923, when he made his major theoretical revision, Freud made one significant attempt to bring his metapsychology up to date. In those of his "Papers on Metapsychology" which have survived, we may note several pertinent additions and emendations. The most important of these was Freud's emphasis on the finding that, although all psychical processes begin in the *Ucs.*, some are not repressed or turned back by the censorship but freely pass into consciousness. Although Freud did not specifically redraw the topographic model in 1915, the implication of his corrected theory for the model is that the mind cannot be shown in terms of two entirely separate systems divided from each other by the repression barrier.[8]

A corollary conclusion (Freud 1915) was that it may be necessary to think of a second censorship between the *Pcs.* and consciousness. If the model is drawn to reflect this concept, consciousness may be shown as a separate system and designated by the symbol *Cs.*

3 Freud's Clinical Theory of 1923: The Tripartite Model

Despite accumulated clinical evidence demonstrating that his models of 1900 could not account for every aspect of mental life, Freud did not return to model building for some time. His theoretical work continued to evolve, however. As Strachey has pointed out, in 1920 Freud shifted his attention back to one of his early observations: the fact that the mechanisms of defense are themselves unconscious (1896). In *Beyond the Pleasure Principle* Freud stated:

It may be that much of the ego is itself unconscious; only a part of it, probably, is covered by the term "preconscious" (p. 19).

In the 1921 edition of this work, Freud changed this statement into one which asserted the point with certainty. He had already mentioned similar views in 1915:

. . . it is not only the psychically repressed that remains alien to consciousness, but also some of the impulses which dominate our ego (p. 192).

Here began the gradual evolution of the usage of the term "ego" to designate more than those aspects of the psychic apparatus which are accessible to consciousness. Freud came to the realization that a meaningful definition of the term required a reformulation.[1] This new theoretical model was elaborated in 1923 in *The Ego and the Id* (see fig. 3).

32

Freud began this work by stating the shortcomings of the topographic model and attempting a redefinition of ego:

> we have formed the idea that in each individual there is a coherent organization of mental processes; and we call this his *ego*. It is to this ego that consciousness is attached; the ego controls the approaches to motility—that is, to the discharge of excitation into the external world; it is the mental agency which supervises all its own constituent processes, and which goes to sleep at night, though even then it exercises the censorship on dreams. From this ego proceed the repressions, too, by means of which it is sought to exclude certain trends in the mind not merely from consciousness but also from other forms of effectiveness and activity (p. 17).

A few years later (1933 [1932]), Freud was to stress that the most important function of the ego is its adaptation of the person to reality (see pp. 75–80).

In 1923, Freud went on to describe the resistances encountered by patients in the course of attempting free association. These resistances are unconscious, that is, the patients are unaware of their operation:

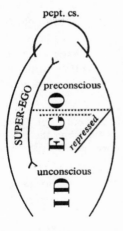

Fig. 3. The Tripartite Model (from *New Introductory Lectures*).

Since . . . there can be no question but that this resistance emanates from [the] ego and belongs to it, we find ourselves in an unforeseen situation. We have come upon something in the ego itself which is also unconscious, which behaves exactly like the repressed—that is, which produces powerful effects without itself being conscious and which requires special work before it can be made conscious (ibid.).

On this basis Freud concluded that "the *Ucs.* does not coincide with the repressed"; therefore, a part of the ego does not belong to the *Pcs.*, but is unconscious.

Freud proceeded to demonstrate that a new concept had to be introduced in order to understand that aspect of mental life connected with the perception of thought processes. This was the idea that thoughts become *Pcs.* only when a thing-presentation has been brought into connection with a word-presentation. It is possible, however, to think wordlessly too, as is done in most dreams. In this case, the optical memory residues of the thing-presentations themselves provide the requisite perceptual quality. Such imagistic thinking is closer to the primary process than are verbal thoughts. Internal sensations or feelings of pleasure and unpleasure must also be transmitted to the perceptual system in order to become conscious. Because the cathectic changes that produce these internal sensations have sensory qualities in themselves, they do not have to pass through the *Pcs.* in order to reach awareness.

Through these arguments Freud had clarified that the *Cs.* is simply a part of the perceptual apparatus. He was now in a position to redefine the ego in a way which includes this perceptual apparatus.

It starts out . . . from the system *Pcpt.* [perceptual system], which is its nucleus, and begins by embracing the *Pcs.*, which is adjacent to the mnemic residues. But, as we have learnt, the ego is also unconscious (p. 23).

Since the perceptual core of memories consists in particular of traces of the body and of its experiences, "the ego is first and foremost a bodily ego" (p. 26).

Freud decided to call "the other part of the mind, into which [the ego] extends and which behaves as though it were *Ucs.*, the 'id'."[2] The conceptualization of the distinction between ego and id was presented in a new pictorial model of the mind. In figure 3 we do not reproduce the original diagram of 1923 but its ultimate elaboration from the *New Introductory Lectures* published a decade later. In this model the ego does not completely envelop the id; it is "not sharply separated from the id; its lower portion merges into it." The repressed also merges into the id but is "cut off sharply from the ego by the resistances of repression" (p. 24).

The ego is that portion of the psychic apparatus which has been modified by the influence of the external world on the id so that in its realm the reality principle has been substituted for the pleasure principle. In subsequent years, Freud modified his views on the development of the ego. In 1937 he stated that both ego and id develop from an originally undifferentiated matrix, a point of view that was to be further elaborated by Hartmann (1939). As for the mechanisms of ego development, Freud said that "the ego is formed to a great extent out of identifications which take the place of abandoned cathexes by the id" (p. 48).

To illustrate the relation of these new systems to one another, Freud invented an analogy that has rightly become famous, that of the man on horseback. The ego/rider was said to borrow its strength from the id/mount; consequently, it is often obliged to carry the will of the id into action as if it were its own. In other words, a rider may merely be pretending to be in control of a runaway horse.

A further elaboration of the new model was necessitated by the recent analytic findings that the faculties of self-criticism and conscience are often unconscious as well. Freud had already made observations of this sort in 1894 in connection with obsessional self-reproaches. In 1916, he had described character types in whom an "unconscious sense of guilt" was crucially important. In the topographic model, the moral sense belongs not to the *Ucs.* but to the *Pcs.* Later evidence that it is in part unconscious as well impelled Freud to make the theoretical innovations in 1923.

The conceptualization of a separate psychic agency for the self-critical functions had actually begun in the paper *On Narcissism* (1914). At that time Freud had postulated the existence of a "differentiating grade" within the ego. He was using the word in the sense of a level or step. The development of this separate functional cluster in the ego was seen as the result of the transformation of infantile narcissism into an "ego ideal." His clinical studies of melancholia and of paranoia within the next decade drew Freud's attention more insistently to this "critical agency" within the mind. He began detailed consideration of the problem in *Group Psychology and the Analysis of the Ego* (1921). However, he did not introduce the term "superego" until 1923.

The origin of this third agency was attributed to that identification with the parents which is brought about by the abandonment of the libidinal attachments to them at the time of the dissolution of the Oedipus complex. Later Freud refined this theory:

a child's superego is in fact constructed on the model not of its parents but of its parents' superego (1933 [1932], p. 67).

The superego is the "heir of the Oedipus complex"; it therefore stands in contrast to the ego, which is the "representative of the external world." The superego is the "representative of the internal world, [of] what is psychical" (1923, p. 36). Freud omitted introducing the superego into his diagram of his model of the mind in *The Ego and the Id*; he did not draw a real "tripartite" model until he published the *New Introductory Lectures*. This is the diagram we have utilized in figure 3. He had described these configurations verbally in 1923, however, when he stated that the superego, in view of its origin, "reaches deep down into the id and for that reason is farther from consciousness than the ego is" (p. 49). This conclusion was buttressed through interpretation of "negative therapeutic reactions" as based on unconscious needs to suffer in order to expiate potential guilt.

The model of mental structure proposed in 1923 and called the "tripartite model" has been the standard one in psychoanalytic usage ever since. Freud restated it on several occasions. In 1933, he stressed the difference between the principle underlying the new model and the one on which the topographic model had been based. The tripartite model represents groupings of mental functions; the topographic one differentiates mental contents according to their accessibility to consciousness. Freud insisted that this distinction should be reflected in consistent differentiation between the ego and the system *Pcpt.-Cs.* The latter is "the outermost superficial portion of the mental apparatus . . . the sense organ of the entire apparatus" (1933 [1932], p. 75).

In the *New Introductory Lectures*, Freud emphasized the dual function of the ego: on the one hand, that of observing and remembering the external world; on the other, that of interposing thought between the id and motor activity. This conception sees the ego as an agency which controls the instinctual drives, albeit never absolutely. Its control must always take into account the possibility provided by external reality as well as the standards of the superego. Freud added this cautionary note:

We cannot do justice to the characteristics of the mind by linear outlines like those in a drawing or a primitive painting, but rather by areas of color melting into one another. . . . After making the separation we must allow that we have separated to merge once more (p. 74).

This is a restatement in terms of the tripartite model of Freud's 1915 amendments to the topographic theory in which he introduced the idea of an area of mental life wherein there is uninterrupted contact between consciousness and the depths.

An Outline of Psychoanalysis (1938) represents Freud's last statement on models of the mind. Here he retained the distinctions between conscious, preconscious, and unconscious mental processes as "psychical qualities." He continued to consider the relations among these processes "from the topographic point of view" (p. 161). The quality of preconsciousness was attributed to the ego alone. The id was thought always to remain unconscious, but the ego and superego could also have this quality. It is in this sharply restricted aspect that the concept of topography survived to the end in Freud's thinking.

A CLINICAL ILLUSTRATION OF THE ADDITION OF STRUCTURAL CONCEPTS TO THE TOPOGRAPHIC ONES

To illustrate the use of the structural theory and of the tripartite model, we will call upon that most complex and fascinating of case histories in the literature of psychoanalysis, the Wolf Man

(Freud 1918 [1914]). Our journals continue to bring us the patient's recollections of his seven decades under analytic scrutiny, and a succession of observers have described his progress since the interruption of his treatment with Freud.[3]

Jones has acclaimed Freud's account of his patient's infantile neurosis as the best of his case histories (1955, pp. 273–78). It was written at the conclusion of the first period of analysis, the summer of 1914, to rebut the arguments of dissidents who were denying the import of early childhood on the adult neurosis. As a result, the focus of the presentation is on childhood events. There are, however, sufficient descriptions of the patient's adult behavior, both in the case history and in subsequent accounts, to permit us to utilize the data for our purposes.

In 1937, Freud gave the following synopsis of the history:

I had taken on the case of a young Russian, a man spoilt by wealth, who had come to Vienna in a state of complete helplessness, accompanied by a private doctor and an attendant. In the course of a few years, it was possible to give him back a large amount of his independence, to awaken his interest in life and to adjust his relations to the people most important to him. But there progress came to a stop. We advanced no further in clearing up the neurosis of his childhood, on which his later illness was based, and it was obvious that the patient found his present position highly comfortable and had no wish to take any step forward which would bring him nearer to the end of his treatment. . . . In this predicament I resorted to the heroic measure of fixing a time-limit for the analysis. . . . At first he did not believe me, but once he was convinced that I was in deadly earnest, the desired change set in. His resistances shrank up, and in these last months of his treatment he was able to reproduce all the memories and to discover all the connections which seemed necessary for understanding his early neurosis and mastering his present one. When he left me in the midsummer of 1914 . . . I believed that his cure was radical and permanent.

. . . I have already reported that I was mistaken. When, towards the end of the war, he returned to Vienna, a refugee and destitute, I had to help him to master a part of the transference which had not been resolved. This was accomplished in a few months. . . . The patient has stayed in Vienna and has kept a place in society, if a humble one. But several times during this period his good state of health has been interrupted by attacks of illness which could only be construed as offshoots of his perennial neurosis. Thanks to the skill of one of my pupils, Dr. Ruth Mack Brunswick, a short course of treatment has on each occasion brought these conditions to an end. . . . Some of these attacks were still concerned with residual portions of the transference; and, where this was so, short-lived as they were, they showed a distinctly paranoid character. In other attacks, however, the pathogenic material consisted of pieces of the patient's life history, which had not come to light while I was analyzing him (1937, pp. 217–18).

In her last note about the patient, in 1945, Dr. Brunswick reported that, after the treatment of the Wolf Man's paranoid illness in 1926–27, he remained well and was relatively productive:

It was after about two years that he returned for the resumption of an analysis as rewarding to me as to him. There was no trace of psychosis or of paranoid trends. Potency disturbances of a neurotic character had occurred in the course of a sudden, violent and repetitive love relation. This time the analysis . . . revealed new material and important, hitherto forgotten memories, all relating to the complicated attachment to [his older sister] the pre-schizophrenic girl. . . . The therapeutic results were excellent (in Fliess 1962, p. 65).

In the last two decades, the Wolf Man has maintained contact with Dr. Muriel Gardiner, who has reported on his major depressive illnesses after his forced retirement at the age of 63 and after the death of his aged mother a few years later.

Even these brief excerpts from reports about the patient's course since he entered analysis with Freud give evidence of psychopathology of kaleidoscopic complexity. This is further compounded if we also consider his earlier life. In the words of Jones (1955):

When he first came to Freud, at the beginning of February, 1910, he was a helpless young man of twenty-three accompanied by a private doctor and valet and unable even to dress himself or face any aspect of life. We know little about his many neurotic symptoms at that time,[4] but his history disclosed that he had suffered from a temporary phobia of wolves at the age of four, followed soon by an obsessional neurosis that lasted till the age of ten. From the age of six he had suffered from obsessional blasphemies against the Almighty, and he initiated the first hour of treatment with the offer to have rectal intercourse with Freud and then to defecate on his head! After the age of ten he was relatively free of suffering, though he had considerable inhibition and eccentricity until an attack of gonorrhea in his seventeenth year when he collapsed with his present illness (pp. 274–75).

It will be sufficient to summarize the historical background in a compressed fashion, as our primary interest is not the genesis of the psychopathology. The patient was the younger child of wealthy landowners who repeatedly left him for long periods and entrusted his upbringing to a succession of domestics. His father suffered from depressions and his mother was in weak health, apparently hypochondriacal in nature. In the summer of his fourth year, his affectionate peasant Nanya was succeeded as his caretaker by a harsh governess. His behavior became rageful and unruly. He had previously been introduced to sexual games by his sister, and his Nanya had threatened him with castration. These active sexual interests were soon replaced by fantasies of being beaten on the penis and by castration fears. The wolf phobia was ushered in by the famous dream of the wolves which Freud was to interpret as the expression of primal scene trauma.[5] This nightmare occurred just before his fourth birthday and constituted his infantile neurosis. After being told the story of Christ's passion at four and a half, the patient became obsessed with the problem of Christ's relationship to God. He identified with Christ as the sexual victim of his own father, an identification facilitated by the fact that he had been born on Christmas day. He became very pious, with many obsessional blasphemous thoughts and compulsive rituals. His affectionate relationship with the father he had formerly admired gradually deteriorated, partly because the latter apparently preferred his sister. The obsessional neurosis seemingly abated, however, in the context of a new relationship to a male tutor; the patient then identified himself with this man. In puberty he once more made sexual overtures to his sister; upon being rebuffed, he turned to a series of servant girls with whom he fell in love in repetitive fashion. His sister committed suicide after the onset of the Wolf Man's emotional illness in adolescence.

In 1914, Freud expressed sharp reservations about the adequacy of the topographic model, the principal theoretical tool then available, for the study of an infantile neurosis:

In the psychology of adults we have fortunately reached the point of being able to give a clearly-worded description of both [mental systems]. With children this distinction leaves us almost completely in the lurch. It is often embarrassing to decide what one would choose to call conscious and what unconscious (1918 [1914], pp. 104–5).

Nevertheless, there were many clinical details which were explained with great economy through the topographic theory. One example is that of an "ingenious dream"—presumably from the last year of the analysis. Freud had made an interpretation connecting an early memory, in which the nursery maid, called Grusha, was scrubbing the floor, with threats of castration. In response, the Wolf Man reported:

"I had a dream," he said, "of a man tearing off the wings of an Espe!"
"*Espe*?" I asked, "What do you mean by that?" "You know, that insect with yellow stripes on its body, that stings." I could now put him right: "So what you mean is a *Wespe* [wasp]." "Is it called a *Wespe*? I really thought it was called an *Espe*!" (Like so many other people he used his difficulties with a foreign language as a screen for symptomatic acts.) But *Espe* was of course a mutilated *Wespe*. The dream said clearly that he was avenging himself on Grusha for her threat of castration (ibid., p. 94).

The interpretation may be difficult to grasp because the dream is based on a pun in Russian: associations to wasps had led to yellow striped pears, and the Russian word for pear is "grusha." Freud's explanation is extremely terse, so that its exact correspondence to the topographic model may be overlooked. It might be amplified in the following manner: the sadistic wish for talion revenge on the person who had threatened the child with castration has persisted as a memory trace of great intensity. It was this repressed *Ucs.* intensity that had been transferred onto a word-presentation in the *Pcs.* Hence the word *Wespe* had its W torn off to create an *Espe*, just as the man was tearing the wings off the insect in the dream. This dream was completely successful in the sense that its ingenious compromise formation permitted the covert fulfillment of a forbidden wish without the production of any anxiety. The foregoing amplification of Freud's interpretation shows that it was possible to grasp the dynamics of this dream through the simple contrast of the two opposing mental systems of topography.

It should be noted that the celebrated nightmare about the wolves could not be explained on the basis of topographic principles. For its interpretation, Freud had to invoke the concept of the repudiation of a wish. This amounted to the conceptualization of a new clinical generalization which was to lead to the higher-level inference that aspects of the conscience are also unconscious (cf. 1918 [1914], p. 42n). In the topographic theory, drive regulating forces do not belong to the system *Ucs.*, so that this new concept transcended the boundaries of his 1900 model of the mind.

The Grusha dream was reported at a stage of the analysis in which resistance was so minimal that the patient succeeded in deciphering the meaning of the dream on his own. In the face of greater resistance, as in the case of the wolf dream, interpretation always has to take into account complex defensive factors, necessitating resort to the theory of intrapsychic conflicts involving the unconscious ego. This approach to psychoanalytic data is that of the tripartite model.

Before turning to those aspects of the case which require the use of the structural theory and the tripartite model for their clarification, we shall demonstrate that the topographic concepts did serve to elucidate data other than successful dreams. To this end, we shall examine the recent report (1968) by the Wolf Man about Freud's interpretations concerning the history of his falling in love with the woman whom he subsequently married. This incident had occurred about a year before the patient came to seek treatment with Freud, at the time he was admitted to Kraepelin's Sanatorium in Munich. The girl was a divorcée who was employed as a nurse at this Sanatorium; she was thus a suitable figure for the transference of the feelings toward the caretaking domestics of the patient's childhood. The Wolf Man fell in love with her on first sight, in the most literal sense. He also realized immediately that she was of Spanish descent.

Freud was able to trace back every determinant of this event to repressed childhood sources. A lifelong fascination with the

Spanish had originated after attending a performance of *Carmen* in St. Petersburg as a child; the role of Carmen had been played by the mistress of the patient's uncle; moreover, this singer's first name was identical with that of the Wolf Man's mother. Precipitously falling in love with a Spanish woman in adult life therefore represented the transference of the repressed incestuous love for his mother. This was a successful compromise formation between *Ucs.* and *Pcs.* forces across the repression barrier.

When it came to eruptions from the depths which were not so easily bound, Freud was ultimately not satisfied with topographic explanations. In *Inhibitions, Symptoms, and Anxiety* he reexamined childhood zoophobias from the perspective of the tripartite model, with a great gain in clarity. In discussing the Wolf Man's phobia, Freud repeated his previous interpretation of the wolf as a father substitute:

the idea of being devoured by the father gives expression, in a form that has undergone regressive degradation, to a passive, tender impulse to be loved by him in a genital-erotic sense (p. 105).

On this basis Freud concluded:

we can see that repression is not the only means which the ego can employ for the purpose of defense against an unwelcome instinctual impulse. If it succeeds in making an instinct regress, it will actually have done it more injury than it could have done by repressing it. Sometimes, indeed, after forcing an instinct to regress in this way, it goes on to repress it (p. 105).

In the case of the Wolf Man, it was passive, erotic impulses toward the father that were principally disposed of by these means; in other instances, hostile impulses form the chief cluster of what needs to be repressed. The motive force of the repression was

fear of impending castration. . . . the little Russian relinquished his wish to be loved by his father, for he thought that a relation of that sort presupposed a sacrifice of his genitals (p. 108).

It was this motivation of fear of castration that led to attempted repudiation of the wish in the dream of the wolves. When the repudiation could not be instantly accomplished, the result was awakening with anxiety. It may therefore be concluded that it is castration anxiety that leads to repression:

In animal phobias, then, the ego has to oppose a libidinal object cathexis coming from the id—a cathexis that belongs either to the positive or to the negative Oedipus complex—because it believes that to give way to it would entail the danger of castration (p. 124).

Freud went on to explain that the formation of a phobia serves the adaptive purpose of diminishing anxiety because a situation in which the danger is an external one can be avoided more easily than an internal danger could be: "the ego is able to escape anxiety by means of avoidance" (p. 126). Freud also noted that the phobias of adults are more complex than those of children in the midst of the Oedipal period. This is so because in adulthood the danger created by giving in to erotic or hostile temptations is that of the punishment meted out by the superego:

But if we ask ourselves what it is that the ego fears from the superego, we cannot but think that the punishment threatened by the latter must be an extension of the punishment of castration (p. 128).

The difference between these clinical conditions, separated by the internalization of the superego, is illustrated in the history of the Wolf Man by his infantile neurosis, that is, his zoophobia, on the one hand, and by the neurotic illness of his later childhood on the other. The chief clinical condition from which he suffered in the latter period was an obsessional neurosis. Freud demonstrated the necessity for going beyond topography to explain the phenomena:

A part of the pious ritual by means of which he eventually atoned for his blasphemies was the command to breathe in a ceremonious manner under certain conditions. Each time he made the sign of the cross he was obliged to breathe in deeply or to exhale forcibly. In his native tongue "breathe" is the same word as "spirit" so that here the Holy Ghost came in. He was obliged to breathe in the Holy Spirit, or to breathe out the evil spirits which he had heard or read about. He ascribed too to these evil spirits the blasphemous thoughts for which he had to inflict such heavy penance on himself (p. 66).

It must be kept in mind that these were interpretations reached during the analysis, not insights available to the child at the time of his illness. As far as the sufferer from the obsessional neurosis is concerned, there is no affective connection between his hostility and his transparently self-punitive behaviors. Such phenomena can only be explained on the basis of the conceptualization of a self-punitive agency which may operate unconsciously. It will be recalled that there is no provision for unconscious self-regulating forces in the topographic theory.

At various times, then, Freud had used topographic concepts to explain some behaviors of the Wolf Man and structural concepts to explain others. In each case, he had selected his theoretical tools appropriately: he applied each model to phenomena pertaining to the developmental phase and to the conditions for which the particular model is most applicable.

4 Freud's Conceptualization of the Unstructured Psyche: The Model of the Reflex Arc

In *The Interpretation of Dreams* Freud stressed the necessity of conceptualizing the functions of the mind in terms of a series of developmental phases; in fact, he had already made this point in the *Project* of 1895. In 1900, he delineated the topographic model in order to clarify conditions in the ultimate phase of such a series, that is, those of adults who have established a repression barrier across which transference phenomena take place. The only other stage in the series which Freud attempted to describe at the time is the initial one, that is, what might be termed the hypothetical conditions he postulated for the newborn. Freud was emphatic about the fact that such a "primary" state of mental functioning is only a theoretical fiction.

The assumption with which Freud started was that the initial function of the mental apparatus is that of avoiding overstimulation. In outlining a "principle of constancy" in 1892, he had already spelled out this assumption:

The nervous system endeavors to keep constant something in its functional relations that we may describe as "the sum of excitation." It puts this precondition of health into effect by disposing associatively of every sensible accretion of excitation or by discharging it by an appropriate motor reaction (pp. 153–54).

If the mental apparatus must avoid overstimulation, the simplest way for it to do so is through immediate motor discharge. Therefore the mind may be conceptualized on the model of a neurologic reflex arc as long as the mind functions in this manner (see fig. 4).

Some confusion about this model has resulted from the fact that Freud's diagram representing this stage of mental organization was then utilized by him for a second purpose, namely, as a first step in his development of the topographic model. Because of the overall gestalt of this diagram, it has sometimes been referred to as the "picket fence" model. It has often been assumed, erroneously, that it portrays the topographic theory, so that the reflex arc model has often not been clearly differentiated from the topographic one. Other writers have attempted to show that the picket fence diagram can be transposed into topographic form by introducing into it the areas of the *Ucs.* and the *Pcs.* We feel that this transposition overlooks the fact that these unconnected theoretical tools were based on entirely different conceptual principles.

To return to the conditions of mental life Freud postulated for the newborn, the most immediate motor discharge available in these circumstances is a direct attempt to reestablish the cessation of stimulation. Such a decrease of stimulation may be attempted through the recathexis of the mnemic image of a previously experienced satisfaction. This short path to the satisfaction of the wish through the reappearance of a percept is called "hallucinatory wish fulfillment." It is a method of seeking discharge that is bound to fail, however; the excitations produced by continuing internal needs can only be discharged by actual experiences of

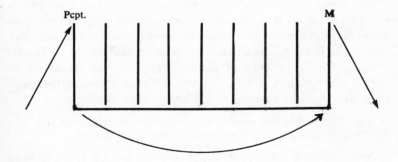

Fig. 4. The Reflex Arc Model (from chap. 7 of
The Interpretation of Dreams).

satisfaction. Therefore it is an essential developmental task to establish a second psychic system which can regulate behavior in such a way that actual satisfactions may be obtained in the world of reality through voluntary motor activity.[1]

Repeated experiences of unpleasure in the form of mounting tension states caused by the ineffectiveness of hallucinatory modes of wish fulfillment necessitate measures to avoid these bitter episodes of frustration. It has not been clearly understood as yet how secondary process thought, which permits the regulation of behavior in a manner that will lead to actual gratification, is developed. At any rate, after this development has taken place, dreams and psychoses may be described as regressive returns to modes of "superseded . . . infantile mental life."

Freud had first noted the "original helplessness of human beings" in the *Project* in 1895. He had concluded that the discharge of excitation caused by endogenous stimuli can only be brought about by alterations of the external world, but that early in life

the human organism is incapable of bringing about the [requisite] specific action. It takes place *by extraneous* help, when the attention of an experienced person is drawn to the child's state (p. 318).

There follows an experience of satisfaction,

and in its repetitions, states of *craving* which have developed into states of *wishing* and states of *expecting* (p. 361).

Freud stated that a functional state in which direct discharge is sought by means of hallucinatory wish fulfillment can only produce disappointment. The lack of actual discharge under such conditions leads to accumulations of excitation which ultimately produce "the experience of pain." These are the conditions he named the "primary process." From them a "secondary process" must develop, one capable of inhibiting direct discharge:

It will be seen that the necessary precondition of the latter is a correct employment of the indication of reality (p. 327).

More recently, this primitive model of mental life has been restated by Rapaport (1951b) who has stressed the heuristic utility of postulating the theoretical fiction of a psychic organization in the newborn akin to the stimulus-response cycle, in which the organism is essentially seen as an "empty" receptacle.

CLINICAL ILLUSTRATIONS OF THE ADDITION OF THE REFLEX ARC MODEL TO PREVIOUS CONCEPTS

Although he was not entirely explicit about it, Freud made use of the reflex arc model in the case history of the Wolf Man in the one instance where this model satisfied the criteria of maximal clarity and economy of explanation: this was in his discussion of the patient's childhood nightmare.[2]

Freud recounted that, late in the analysis, the patient returned to this dream and realized that the tree on which the wolves were sitting outside his window had been a Christmas tree:

He now knew that he had dreamt the dream shortly before Christmas and in expectation of it. . . . It was immediately before his fourth birthday. He had gone to sleep, then, in tense expectation of the day which ought to bring him a double quantity of presents. We know that in such circumstances a child may easily anticipate the fulfillment of his wishes. So it was already Christmas in his dream; the content of the dream showed him his Christmas box, the presents which were to be his were hanging on the tree. But instead of presents they had turned into wolves, and the dream ended by his being overcome by fear of being eaten by the wolf (probably his father), and by his flying for refuge to his nurse (p. 35).

Freud's interpretation of the nature of the wish represented by the ravenous wolves has already been mentioned in our discussion of zoophobia. He assumed that the child became filled with sexual excitement of a passive homosexual type, derived from a previous primal scene exposure. Without spelling this out in 1914, Freud was therefore describing a situation of psycho-economic disturbance, the "accumulation of amounts of stimulation which require to be disposed of" (1926 [1925], p. 137). This is the situation of danger of overstimulation:

. . . the ego is reduced to a state of helplessness in the face of an excessive tension due to need . . . anxiety is then generated (ibid., p. 141).[3]

In this sense, then, the nightmare of the wolves created the "actual neurotic core" of the Wolf Man's psychoneurosis:[4]

> The activation of the picture . . . [of the primal scene] . . . operated not only like a fresh event, but like a new trauma, like an interference from outside analogous to the seduction (1918 [1914], p. 109).

Another example of the traumatic state, best understood in terms of the reflex arc model, occurs in Freud's discussion of the case of Daniel Paul Schreber (1911), and in particular around the events surrounding the outbreak of this patient's psychosis. We cannot improve on the following brief summary of the case history provided by Jones (1955):

> The patient, Dr. Schreber, had an attack of nervous disorder in 1885, and was for fifteen months in a clinic under the care of a distinguished psychiatrist, Professor Flechsig of Leipzig. At the end of this time he was discharged, full of gratitude and affection, completely cured, and he remained so for the next ten years. His condition during this attack was labeled "hypochondria."
> Then, only three weeks after assuming his responsible position as *Senatspräsident*, he fell ill with a far more serious affliction. This time he was under care for six years, when he was discharged in a perfectly normal mental state except for certain fixed delusions. This serious illness had two distinct phases. In the first one, which lasted about a year, he suffered from extremely distressing delusions of persecution. He imagined he was being the victim of horrible homosexual assaults at the hands of his former physician, Flechsig, who before long was aided and abetted by God himself. In the second phase he had voluptuously accepted this destiny, but at the hands of God. This was accompanied by various religious and megalomanic ideas according to which he would become a feminine savior of the world and breed a new and superior race of human beings (p. 269).

The outbreak of psychosis had been ushered in by a series of dreams leading to orgasm. This condition was quickly followed by a delusional state, "while simultaneously a high degree of hyperaesthesia was observable—a great sensitiveness to light and noise" (Freud 1911c, p. 13). We believe that these observations indicate that the patient's capacity to bind excitation had been overwhelmed, that is, that these phenomena are best understood in terms of the reflex arc model. The state of overstimulation was vividly described in Schreber's *Memoirs*:

I was overtaxed mentally. I started to sleep badly. . . . During several nights, a recurrent cracking noise in the wall of our bedroom became noticeable at shorter or longer intervals; time and again it woke me as I was about to go to sleep. . . . I suffered from palpitation so that walking up only a moderate incline caused attacks of anxiety. . . . I spent the night almost without sleep and once left the bed in an attack of anxiety in order to make preparation for a kind of suicide attempt. . . . The next morning my nerves were badly shattered; the blood had gone from my extremities to my heart, my mood was gloomy in the extreme. . . . in the following days I could not occupy myself in any way . . . my mind was occupied almost exclusively with thoughts of death. . . . I was already in a highly excited state, in a fever of delirium so to speak (pp. 38–39).

Although Schreber attempted some retrospective explanations, the psychological meaning of the stimuli which had overloaded his mental apparatus seems less significant than the economic factor of the overstimulation itself. The next phase in his clinical course was that of a "hallucinatory insanity," as Schreber's psychiatrist called it, akin to what has been described above as hallucinatory wish fulfillment.

SUMMARY OF FREUD'S THREE MODELS OF THE MIND

We have now reviewed the three models explicitly drawn by Freud to illustrate his various conceptualizations of mental functioning. The three models fall into two types: one is applicable to the state of the psyche at the hypothetical inception of its functioning; the other two are applicable to psychic functioning at the stage of full structural differentiation. The former is the reflex arc model; the latter are the topographic and tripartite ones.

Our historical survey highlights certain general issues of model building. In our opinion, it demonstrates the fact that models may be constructed in a variety of ways. The principle of their organization may be chosen on an ad hoc basis, provided the model remains faithful to the concepts it is intended to portray. In other words, it can and should be conceived so that it may focus on those aspects of function which are felt to be the most important ones in a given instance. In 1900, Freud had chosen to construct the topographic model on the principle of spotlighting the differential accessibility of various mental contents to consciousness. This was a cogent choice because the phenomena he was then trying to understand had the common property of being unable to gain access to consciousness directly. In contrast, the 1923 tripartite model was based on the central idea of disparate functional units comprising an apparatus; this choice was dictated by Freud's need at the time to understand observations bearing on various sets of typical intrapsychic conflicts.

Our survey has also revealed an important lacuna in psychoanalytic theory: the absence of any effort to delineate useful concepts and models for those stages of mental development which lie between the end points that Freud had dealt with. New conceptual tools are needed to clarify functional states which occur between those of the newborn psyche and the fully differentiated psyche.[5] An effort to outline some tentative concepts and models applicable to this range of function will be made in the following chapters.

5 On the Unformulated Segment of Psychoanalytic Theory: The Emerging Psychology of the Self

Waelder's principle of multiple function (1936) was the metapsychological concept which first called for a new perspective within psychoanalytic theory: the study of the psychic apparatus as a mediator of adaptation. The concept of the psyche as the possessor of the higher functions of anticipation and synthesis goes beyond the boundaries of the structural theory (cf. Hartmann 1939). In this as well as other ways, psychoanalytic psychology has increasingly come to be an ego psychology which has burst the confines of the original Freudian conceptualizations contained in *The Ego and the Id*. The need for novel conceptual tools to handle these evolutions in theory has thus far gone unrecognized, except for Modell's call for a new theory, quoted above in chapter 1.

Nonetheless, the progressive broadening of the ego concept has recently come under critical scrutiny. Several issues have been raised that cast doubt on the viability of these extrapolations from the structural theory. Klein (1968) has concluded that psychoanalysis faces a choice between a model of the ego as a supraordinate regulatory system on the one hand, and, on the other, the definition of the ego as a subordinate agency within the mind concerned only with psychological conflict as one of the levers of the multiple functions of action.

We wish to emphasize that in this monograph the term "ego" will be used only in the sense implied by the second of these alternatives; that is, as a functional unit of the psyche which is

53

either in conflict or in equilibrium with the drives. In other words, our usage will be in conformity with that of Freud in 1923. We believe that much confusion will be avoided if "ego," a construct belonging to the structural theory and the tripartite model, were not utilized in referring to functions which are more fruitfully viewed outside the sphere of intersystemic conflicts—that is, those among ego, id, and superego. It is particularly cogent to recall that a model not involving conflict is implied whenever the concept of secondary autonomy is invoked. Because the tripartite model does not refer to such conditions, it is theoretically misleading to include conflict-free behaviors within the scope of ego psychology.

The point of view we are espousing is merely the translation into more precise theoretical terminology of the concept of an area of the personality in which there is uninterrupted contact with the depths, separate from the area of transferences, as proposed by Kohut and Seitz (1963) and as previously outlined by Freud in 1915.[1] Freud's metaphor for the id and the ego, that of a horse and its rider, can be modified to portray these spheres of behavior through an analogous image: that of a centaur. Whenever mental activity is centaur-like, it partakes equally of drive motivations and drive-regulating ones. This is the state of the child's mental organization prior to the definitive differentiation of the ego from the id, which occurs with the resolution of the Oedipus complex.[2] When such circumstances lacking in conflict predominate in adult mental life, the use of the word "ego" to designate the regulatory system of the personality introduces confusion by assigning a second meaning to the term which differs from that given to it within the structural theory. We prefer to find a different terminological solution to account for phenomena such as perception, memory, thinking, affectivity, and so on. These are more than "ego functions" if the term "ego" is to retain the meaning required by the structural theory, that is, the organization of defenses against the drives. In his discussion of secondary autonomy, Hartmann (1939) clearly indicates that he extends the scope of psychoanalysis beyond the areas of mental function covered by the tripartite model. The assignment of supraordinate functions such as integration or synthesis to the system Ego certainly does violence to Freud's original conceptualization of 1923, that of the rider. To insist on clear differentiation between these divergent usages of the ego concept is therefore no semantic quibbling.

When the psychic organization has not yet been differentiated into the tripartite structure it *typically* assumes with the resolution of the Oedipus complex, or when this differentiation has been lost through regression, the subsidiary concepts of the structural theory become poorly applicable. It is imprecise to designate functions such as memory or perception as "ego functions." Perhaps even the defenses of these archaic modes of psychic organization should not be conceived of primarily as drive-regulating functions, in view of the fact that they are most often concerned with the handling of external dangers; that is, they are defenses against perceptions rather than against instinctual drives.

In short, we are in favor of a strategy of retrenchment for the ego concept, on the basis of the greater relevance of alternative constructs for many of the situations to which it has been applied. G. Klein (1968) has also come to the conclusion that psychoanalytic psychology has more to gain from this direction of theory building than from the available alternative, that of "continuing to explicate a model of the ego as a regulatory mechanism—building into it more detailed process assumptions to implement its heretofore implied, but unspecified reifications."

Dissatisfaction with an established theory remains sterile unless something of greater utility is offered in its place. We have therefore assumed the obligation to find suitable analytic concepts to replace ego psychology in those areas of mental life in which the latter is not truly cogent. In our survey of Freud's theoretical work, we have already found one instance, that of his reflex arc model of 1895 and 1900, of a useful conceptual tool applicable to the undifferentiated psychic organization. We have also found a segment of psychic life, the area between these primitive beginnings and the fully differentiated state represented by the tripartite model, for which psychoanalytic theory has not yet formulated any model. We shall now attempt to propose a suitable conceptualization for these intermediate stages of psychic organization. Our attempts will have to be guided by our estimate of the overriding problems of psychic functioning at these intermediate stages of differentiation and by the best existing psychoanalytic conceptualizations of these problems.[3] The task of devising a model which would optimally illuminate these stages of psychic life is one of great complexity because of the wide variety of modes of operation resulting from the simultaneous maturation of many crucial aspects of function. In her most extensive work on developmental psychology, *Normality and Pathology in Childhood* (1965), Anna Freud chose the developmental line "from dependency to emotional self-reliance and adult object relationships" (p. 64) as the principal and prototypical one. In our view, this choice reflects the overwhelming importance of the actual transactions between the infant and his environment for the organization of the personality. As Anna Freud stated, this is "a sequence for which the successive stages of libido development (oral, anal, phallic) merely form the inborn, maturational base" (pp. 64–65).

Psychoanalytic psychology has arrived at this viewpoint relatively late in its own development. The explicit study of the relation of the self to the world of its objects did not begin until 1914, with Freud's study *On Narcissism*. In this paper, he summed up his conclusions from the investigation of the narcissistic neuroses. In his terms, these were the psychopathological entities closest in their mode of psychic organization to the more archaic phases of childhood psychic life. It has, of course, been a general assumption of psychoanalytic psychology that elucidation of psychopathology in adult life will reveal some features which, although they have been altered in certain ways in the course of maturation, still echo in certain other essentials the childhood modes of functioning which characterized their inception. The study of the narcissistic neuroses therefore promised to yield inferences which could cautiously be applied to the development of the mind in earlier childhood.

The fact that the narcissistic neuroses were found not to be analyzable when psychoanalysis was first applied to them thus became an historical factor that may have delayed the appreciation of the importance of object relations. The psychoanalytic observation of adult neurotics yielded data about intrapsychic conflicts, principally those of the Oedipus complex. In these conditions, actual object relations, in Anna Freud's sense of the provision of need satisfactions, do not play a significant part. The psychoanalysis of children, which might have called Freud's attention to the imperative need of children to have others perform for them the functions which their immature psychic equipment cannot yet manage on its own (see Kohut 1966), had not yet been attempted. The only child treated by Freud, Little Hans, was directly observed by him during a single consultation.[4] With the gradual expansion in the scope of psychoanalytic treatment and the development of child analysis, we have accumulated a considerable body of data bearing on the earliest phases of developmental psychology. These data have been supplemented by direct observations of children inaccessible to psychoanalytic treatment (see Hartmann 1950).

Nevertheless, in *On Narcissism*, Freud had already focused on the issue of object relations as a cardinal one for the study of the less than fully differentiated psyche.[5] It has not been generally appreciated that this constitutes the implicit utilization of a model of mental functioning organized on the principle of depicting changes in object relations, although Freud neither drew such a diagram nor gave explicit emphasis to the theoretical significance of his discussion. As a matter of fact, this significance was extremely difficult to grasp because of Freud's use of ambiguous and confusing terminology, particularly that of the term *das Ich*. Hartmann (1956) was the first to resolve this confusion by demonstrating that for the pre-1923 period within Freud's writings, this term should be translated as "the self," that is, one's own person.[6] Consequently, narcissism was to be understood as "the libidinal cathexis of one's own person, as opposed to that of the objects" (Hartmann 1956, p. 288).

Freud differentiated the narcissistic neuroses from the transference neuroses on the basis of the distinction that libidinal frustration leads to different responses in those two kinds of patients. Persons with transference neuroses respond to frustration by investing libido in fantasied objects, that is, in intrapsychic representations of objects. In similar circumstances, persons with narcissistic neuroses show a withdrawal of libido onto the self. Freud postulated that such a cathexis of the self with libido constitutes a transformation of the drive itself from "object libido" to "narcissistic libido." He understood a change in this direction as a regressive one and assumed that it was ordinarily reversible. His conclusion about normal development was that with the secure differentiation of the self from the objects, there is a parallel change from "primary narcissism," or exclusively narcissistic libido, to a progressive predominance of object libido, and that this change is a relatively stable one. Freud pictured this process as one of tentative steps, however, which he described through one of his most telling metaphors, that of the pseudopodia of an amoeba moving forward to enclose an object and then withdrawing from it. This verbal analogy might be considered as a model of mental function portraying object relations. It will readily lend itself to graphic representation (see fig. 5).[7]

These are the modest beginnings from which the psychoanalytic theory of object relations evolved. Lichtenstein (1964) may have been the first to discern that Freud's theory of narcissism, that is, his psychology of the self, "contains as radical a revolution" as did his introduction of the structural theory in 1923. It was perhaps the production of this second revolutionary advance in psychoanalytic theory within less than a decade which made the exploitation of the breakthrough of 1914 so difficult: the structural theory is relevant to those aspects of psychic life which occupy the forefront in the treatment of the transference neuroses, so that its importance was grasped more quickly than that of narcissism, albeit even the former advance took several decades to triumph. In the meantime, object relations theory developed slowly, without consensus, and without the necessary metapsychological precision. The history of this process need not be reviewed here; it may suffice to recall that the need for a theory of object relations was felt most keenly by those analysts who had clinical

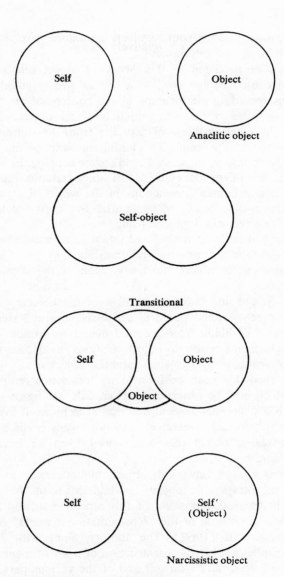

Fig. 5. Illustration of the types of object relations.

experience with persons with relatively immature psychic organization—children and psychotics.[8]

The lack of precision in the theory of object relations may have been caused by the need to arrive at two essential sets of distinctions regarding the meaning of the concept of an "object." The first of these is the differentiation of an object as a real person in the external world of actuality from the representation of that person in the mind. The initial meaning of the concept of object relations, as in Anna Freud's statement of the developmental line from dependency to "adult object relationships," concerns the actual human transactions in the world of actuality. It may be appropriate briefly to summarize the steps she has enumerated along this developmental line.

1. Biological unity of mother and infant in a narcissistic milieu.
2. A need-fulfilling, anaclitic relationship.
3. Attainment of object constancy, even in the face of frustration.
4. Ambivalent and sadistic control over the object.
5. An object-centered phase of possessiveness and rivalry.
6. Transfer of libido from parental figures to groups.
7. Preadolescent return to object relations of archaic types.
8. Adolescent struggle to shed infantile object ties.

It will be seen that each position along this series refers to behaviors which may be observed from an external frame of reference. Such a phenomenological description is by itself insufficient for metapsychological assessment. Psychoanalysis needs a parallel set of phases in object relations viewed from an intrapsychic vantage point.

From this second viewpoint, object relations refer to the significance of intrapsychic objects as laid down in the memory system. The clearest exposition of this aspect of mental function is the conceptualization of the "representational world" by Sandler and Rosenblatt (1962). The authors, along with Jacobson (1964), emphasize that the construction of a set of mental representations of the child's own self and of the various persons who people his universe is a lengthy developmental process.[9] The models of psychic functioning we wish to construct for the era of mental life intermediate between the reflex arc and tripartite modes of organization will refer to this representational world of intrapsychic objects and self-representations.

The second distinction which must be made before a metapsychologically precise discussion of object relations can be attempted is the differentiation of object relations in general from the issue of object love. This theoretical advance has been taken by the recent work of Heinz Kohut on narcissism (1966, 1968, 1971). Kohut has stressed that objects needed to supply functions which are not yet available to the immature psyche will be experienced in the intrapsychic world as if they were parts of the self. In terms of Freud's libidinal formulations, these need-fulfilling objects are invested with narcissistic libido. Consequently, Kohut has proposed that they be designated as "self-objects." The relations of the child with these archaic objects cannot properly be assigned to the developmental line of the vicissitudes of object love; rather, they belong within the province of the development of narcissism.[10] The line of development of object love proper can only begin after the secure differentiation of the self from the object. In the series of stages of object relations described by Anna Freud, this point is reached with the attainment of object constancy. Prior to this achievement, as Kohut has stated (1971), objects are not loved for their attributes, which are at best dimly recognized. It should be emphasized that cognitive differentiation between the self and an object in the external world is achieved much earlier, usually before the end of the first year of life; this corresponds to the change from the original mother-infant symbiosis to the stage of the need-fulfilling object along Anna Freud's schema of object relations. Long after the achievement of this cognitive distinction, the child continues to utilize the object as part of his narcissistic world. Modell (1968) states this in terms of the child's continuing need to create illusory substitutes that he can control in place of the actual mother who has an independent center of volition. Following the persuasive clinical observations of Winnicott (1951), Modell prefers to call this type of object relationship a "transitional object." By utilizing such fantasies of omnipotence, the infant is enabled to preserve in one aspect of his mind his illusion of symbiosis.

Modell's conceptualization implied that, at this stage of psychic life, the child routinely tolerates gross contradictions in his mental organization. He is simultaneously separate from the object and fused with it insofar as the object is needed to function as a part of the self, that is, as a self-object. A different aspect of this mode of organization has received more emphasis in the psychoanalytic literature. This is the lack of integration of the memories of gratifying and frustrating experiences with the object, leading to the persistence, side by side, of "good" and "bad" imagoes referable to the same object (cf. Segal 1969). Because of the child's inability to view the object in its totality, these archaic imagoes are often called "part objects."

Whether archaic self-objects are referred to as "transitional" (in an extension of Winnicott's conceptualization from the preferred possessions of young children to their human relations which have similar meanings) or as "part-objects" may be a matter of taste. In any case, Modell (1968) has shown that these varied object imagoes are gradually sorted out realistically, and, with the achievement of stable reality testing,[11] they are consolidated into whole objects with stable characteristics. Modell points out that this is the step that opens the way to loving and hating the same person.

Modell's discussion of object relations is focused on the intrapsychic world; it also manages to avoid the confusion of this early phase of development with later stages, which are properly described in terms of a mind differentiated into the agencies of the structural theory. The failure to make this distinction has defeated the attempts of Melanie Klein and her school to develop a workable theory of object relations (cf. Segal 1969); the lack of theoretical clarity in the writings of Fairbairn (1954) may be due to the same confusion. Modell, too, fails to attain the necessary clarity in his acceptance of the view that cognitive differentiation of self from object marks the emergence of the self as a cohesive entity. Kohut's contribution, which differentiates self-objects from those invested with true object libido, makes it possible for the first time to clarify not only the evolving sequence of the child's objects but also the complementary issue, that of the development of his self.[12]

The central clinical discovery of Kohut's study of narcissistic personality disturbances (1971) has been that of the overriding importance of the attainment of a sense of the cohesion of the self. It is this state of consolidation that other authors (Jacobson 1964, Lichtenstein 1961) have referred to as a stable sense of identity. Failure to achieve cohesion of the self characterizes various forms of severe psychopathology. In the analyzable types of narcissistic disturbance delimited by Kohut, this unity is still vulnerable to fragmentation under stress. Regressive fragmentation of the sense of the wholeness of the personality corresponds to the clinical states Freud called "splits in the ego" (1927). In this instance, Freud clearly returned to a usage of the word "ego" not consonant with its definition within the structural theory. We propose, therefore, that the concept would be more appropriately designated by the term "splitting of the self."

As we have noted previously, it was Hartmann who pointed out that many of Freud's references to *das Ich* must be understood as "one's own person." Hartmann confined his own usage of the term "self" to a nonpsychological one, that is, one referring only to the totality of the person. Jacobson (1964) has also opted against the use of this term for a psychological construct. Kohut, on the other hand, has shown the dynamic and genetic significance of the organized system of memories commonly designated as the self-representations. In our view, the complex controversies in recent psychoanalytic theory around the concept of identity certainly suggest that there has been an unfilled need within the theory on this issue. The system of memories which constitutes the self-representation is an organized and enduring psychological constellation which continues to exert an active dynamic influence on behavior. It is insufficient to conceptualize these memories as mental contents alone; they are more than the passively recorded percepts of the activities of one's own person in the past. By virtue of their continuing dynamic effects, they must be understood, in addition, as an actuality in the real world—the organized personality as a whole. The simplest designation for this is the term self.

Many authors have preferred to utilize the term "identity" to designate the enduring organization of the personality which is achieved in the course of development (cf. Lichtenstein 1961, 1964; Jacobson 1964). We agree with Kohut's rejection of this term on the grounds that its usage is an attempt to straddle the gap between two disciplines, social and individual psychology, without really belonging to either. Erikson (1959) has compounded the terminological muddle by introducing the variant "ego-identity" to designate the ultimate maturation of the sense of self in adolescence. Needless to say, we deplore his grafting of the language of ego psychology onto issues that do not pertain to it. We believe, moreover, that the term "identity" fails to denote with sufficient clarity that what is in question is not simply a set of remembered transactions from the past. Identity may be a useful term if restricted in its usage to the description of the self in its social field. However, there is a danger in using "identity" as a psychoanalytic term. Confusion may result from externalizing problems which pertain to the formation of the archaic, nuclear self (Kohut 1971) onto the social context of the patient in adult life by referring to them as "identity problems."

The utilization of the construct "self" has been hampered not only by the inherent difficulty of grasping the subtle idea that the organization of the personality as a whole may be an important developmental achievement of early childhood but also by the semantic problems created by attempts to superimpose this concept on the tripartite model of the mind. It may not be possible to find a place for the self within the scheme of the ego since ego is a concept at a different level of abstraction, referring to a narrower segment of behavior and cogent with regard to behaviors that do not begin operation until long after the unification of self. In this connection, it may be pertinent to recall the recommendation of Grinker (1957):

we need a term to apply to a supraordinate process which functions in integrating sub-systems, including the many identifications that constitute the ego, the ego-ideal, and superego, and in organizing behavior into available social roles (p. 389).

We submit that the concept of self developed by Kohut and extended here can also meet Rapaport's demand (1960) for a theory

concerning the relation of the "self" or of "identity" to the psychoanalytic theory of psychological functions in general and of ego functions in particular (p. 136).[13]

If we apply the clinical discoveries of Kohut in the realm of narcissistic personality disturbances to an expansion of developmental psychology, we may conclude that the phase of self-cohesion must be preceded by one in which aspects of the self are not yet unified. We believe that Freud was alluding to this state of organization when he postulated a phase of "separate instinctual activity," or autoerotism (1911). This phase was followed in his schema of libidinal development by one of "narcissism," a phase in which the infant takes his own self as a love object. This may very well correspond to the stage of the cohesive self in Kohut's terminology.

These considerations underscore the utility of Glover's conception of separate ego nuclei (1932, 1943) in the early phase of psychic life. In line with our previous comments about terminology, we feel that it would be preferable to modify Glover's designation and to speak of "nuclei of the self." It is from such antecedent nuclei that the cohesive, whole self is gradually built, in parallel with the realistic sorting out of the variety of part objects into cohesive wholes. In later stages of psychic organization, when the loss of self-cohesion no longer threatens actual fragmentation, the differentiated ego may be able to utilize the regressive pathway of splitting of the self in the service of defense. This is the process that was called "disavowal" by Freud (1923). When this defense is in operation, the nonrecognized or unacknowledged aspects of mental activity do not lie behind a repression barrier; they are separated from the acknowledged parts of the self by a failure of synthesis or integration.

The issues concerning the gradual differentiation of whole objects and the unification of the cohesive self predominate in the mental life of the child, starting with the child's capacity to make cognitive distinctions between the self and the external world. They continue to be most pertinent until the final relinquishment of the utilization of self-objects. It is the formation of the superego, in consequence of the development of the castration complex, which permits the internalization of self-regulating functions and thus renders the child capable of relating to objects solely in terms of loving and hating, without narcissistic merger. Thenceforth, the issues of self and object relations gain primary relevance only in those regressive states which reproduce the childhood symbiosis with objects.[14]

After the formation of the superego and the differentiation of the ego, it is, of course, the tripartite model which illuminates mental life most adequately. At the other end of the maturational scale, however, in the conflict-free sphere to which the concept of intrapsychic conflicts embodied in the structural theory does not apply, it may once more be useful to think of the organization of the self, or of the personality as a whole, as the issue of cardinal importance. From this perspective, it may even be legitimate to conceive of the expectable tripartite structure of the psyche in conflict as one of the modes in which the self may be organized. We are suggesting that a developmental line of the self may be divided into three major phases: that of the self in formation, capped by a state of cohesiveness; that of the self in conflict among its drives, its internalized standards, and its reality sense; and that of the self beyond conflict, the expansion of permanent capacities which make themselves felt in behavior through internal harmony, centaur-like. This epigenetic view of the self needs to be elaborated in detail in future studies.[15]

We may now be in a position to suggest a model to portray the vicissitudes of self and objects during the phases of mental life in which these are the most important psychological issues. We have chosen to elaborate this model by building upon Freud's metaphor for object relations, that of the amoeba with its pseudopodia. The graphic representations we shall suggest are to be understood as portrayals of the representational world—not of actualities in the interpersonal sphere or the social field, but as intrapsychic conditions.

The model will be built up from units which portray the self in relation to one of its objects. The various types of object relations possible are illustrated in figure 5. The mature love relationship of a whole self to a whole object is shown in terms of two self-enclosed entities in proximity. Written labels serve to identify subject and object; these labels can also differentiate objects chosen on the anaclitic basis from those selected because they somehow mirror the self ("narcissistic objects" in Freud's terminology). The former have simply been labeled "object"; the latter bear the designation "self-object." The utilization of self-objects is shown graphically by merging the circles which stand for each person, in analogy to the hyphenation in the written symbol for this type of object relationship. Finally, the use of a transitional object is drawn in terms of circles symbolizing self and other in close proximity, each of them partially open to a third entity, the transitional object, which overlaps them both and thereby joins them.

In the actual model of the mind based on vicissitudes of self and objects, the representational world is portrayed by choosing among these symbols of various types of object relations those which best correspond to the clinical situation of the moment. In figure 6, we offer but two such possibilities; the great variety of configurations encountered in practice will be further illustrated when we apply the self-object model to case materials (see chapters 8 through 10). Figure 6a shows mental functioning on the basis of a cohesive self in relation to a variety of whole objects, some chosen on an anaclitic, others on a narcissistic, basis. This is, in fact, a picture of object relations after the cessation of the utilization of self-objects, that is, at a time when the self-object model is no longer most germane for the actual issues of mental functioning. In the transitional stage, both relations of the kind pictured in figure 6a and others involving the diagram of

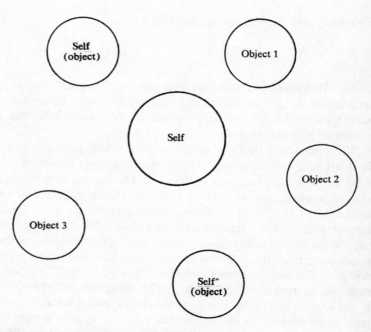

a. Whole self related to series of whole objects.

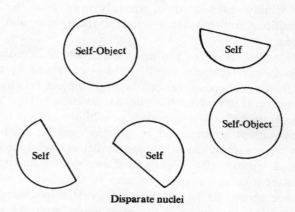

Disparate nuclei

b. Model of disparate nuclei of self and objects.

Fig. 6. Models of intrapsychic representations of self and objects.

self-objects as drawn in figure 5 must coexist. In addition, transitional objects are also likely in the representational world at this stage.

By contrast to the mature conditions portrayed by the previous model, figure 6b is a picture of the representational world prior to the formation of a cohesive self. There are a number of self-objects, each with different qualities; this is indicated on the diagram by the use of varying typographical styles for labeling each object, implying the lack of integration among the various aspects of these objects. Similarly, varied aspects of the self coexist without integration; these are also labeled through a variety of typefaces. In order to indicate that each aspect of the self or nucleus is but a partial one, the symbol used is not a complete circle but only a segment of one.

Impending fragmentation of a cohesive self into its antecedent nuclei might be represented graphically by drawing the self as a complete circle and then subdividing it into a number of segments each of which could bear a different label. Such a regressive shift would ordinarily be accompanied by a set of additional changes in functioning, outside of the sphere of object relations. We would prefer to conceptualize such events in a broader framework, to be presented in the next chapter.

II | The Hierarchical Model

6 Developmental Lines in Interaction

We have now reviewed the clinical theories in common use since their introduction by Freud as well as some others that we feel were implicit within his work. All of these theories share the characteristic of embodying the dynamic and structural points of view of metapsychology. An additional metapsychological point of view, the economic one, could be added to them by suitable modification and additions. The organization of data from the genetic viewpoint is not clearly presented by Freud in any of the illustrative models devised for these theories, despite the fact that genetic factors are essential for the understanding of clinical material.

The desirability, then, of devising a model of mental life built around the course of psychological development itself is evident. This model should be capable of portraying the simultaneous possibilities for progressive and regressive modes of functioning in an explicit manner. An implicit understanding of genetic antecedents for existing mental conditions that can be assumed in every psychoanalytic theory is not sufficient for gaining a clear picture either of their development or of the potential fluctuations they are likely to undergo.

In choosing an organizing principle for our exposition, which utilizes primarily the chronology of development, we are applying to the study of *overall* mental functioning a common principle which psychoanalysis has used in studying various *discrete* mental functions.[1] This approach was first used by Freud in the *Three*

Essays on the Theory of Sexuality (1905). He presented the development of the libido as an epigenetic series. The principle was adopted by Ferenczi and named "lines of development" in 1913, when he presented his work on the development of the sense of reality. The most consistent advocate of this approach has been Anna Freud (1965), and we have already discussed the theoretical significance of the epigenetic view in chapter 1.

Psychic development is progressive structuralization. Therefore, in attempting to construct a developmental model, we must outline the acquisition of mental structure, in the broadest sense of the term. In that sense, "structure" signifies enduring function. However, as Rapaport has emphasized (1960), "structural determiners of behavior . . . are *relatively* permanent" [our italics]. The question of the relative stability of various mental functions, "of their reversibility or irreversibility . . . vis à vis inner or outer stress" has been most cogently studied by Hartmann (1952). He has warned that newly acquired functions "show a high degree of reversibility in the child" (p. 177). He has also differentiated "apparatuses of primary autonomy" from those of "secondary autonomy." The former are structures which are relatively stable from their inception; the latter acquire stability only gradually. This is a novel way of differentiating inborn from acquired structures. The question of autonomy, raised by Hartmann as early as 1939, must be dealt with in any developmental model, at least with regard to the most important functions of the psyche.

As we have described in the introductory chapter, maturation toward secondary autonomy can be indicated on a developmental schema by the vertical axis of a rectangular coordinate graph (see fig. 1). By organizing it in this manner, we can follow Glover's recommendation (1950):

what we call in the structural sense organization of mind is not to be thought of merely as a series of *superimposed* developmental levels. There is, to use a spatial image, a vertical as well as a horizontal development of the apparatus (p. 374).

Glover has also stressed that all functional systems continue to operate concurrently throughout life once they have been formed.

He called for the simultaneous examination of a number of discrete functions in a developmental map of mental functioning. Actually, this program echoes Freud's statement in a letter of 1933: "The next psychological 'map' would have to be in more detail than the one we have today" (Weiss 1970).

The map we are about to draw will not be as detailed as it ideally needs to be; in order to preserve clarity of exposition, we must content ourselves with outlining those lines of development which we consider to be most essential. Even with this limitation, should we wish to show all of the alternative modes available for the accomplishment of a given mental task simultaneously, the diagram will still be somewhat complex. To illustrate this point, let us return to the example we utilized to explain the concept of epigenesis in chapter 1, the developmental line of the libido. It is well known that some portions of the libido do not participate in the general progression of development (cf. Hartmann and Kris 1945). Oral, anal, and phallic wishes will be found in people who have already achieved genital primacy. An adequate developmental model must be able to show all of these varied strands of the sexual drive operating concurrently. Moreover, some of these early, "primitive" functions persist in their original form, unaltered, while other portions undergo "changes of function." Such changes will be indicated along the vertical axis of the rectangular coordinates of the diagram.

As development progresses, there is increasing elaboration of potentialities for function at both more primitive and more mature levels, with or without "change of function." This elaboration may be shown on the model through the graphic device of layering. That is to say, at each developmental phase, beneath the division indicating the modes of function typical for that stage, we will include a listing of all of the previously utilized modes, each of which may still be activated. Such activation may occur as a result of regression under stress or in altered states of consciousness, in the service of either adaptation or creativity, and in a number of other circumstances.

The unfolding of human personality is an intricate process involving various achievements made possible by phase specific maturational progress in a number of independent functions. The choice of those lines of development which are to be included in a hierarchical model is therefore made without rigid or absolute criteria. The suggestions we will put forward at this time are to be regarded as tentative and flexible. These selections have been guided by the nosology of behaviors that are expected to be differentiated from each other by means of the model.[2]

The clinical orientation of the rationale in the choice of the functions to be included in the model leads to concentration on areas which are sensitive to the results of interaction with the environment. There will be less concern with sequences in maturation which have more or less invariable patterns of development. For example, we shall not include the development of the aggressive drives or of the apparatuses of primary autonomy, on the assumption that these relatively invariant developmental patterns either usually make but a small contribution to diagnostic assessment or must await future clarification of their significance by psychoanalytic research.

THE INTERACTION OF TWO DEVELOPMENTAL LINES: THE TYPICAL SITUATIONS OF DANGER AND OBJECT RELATIONS

We shall begin the exposition of the interaction of developmental lines by returning to the typical situations of danger which we presented in chapter 1. Situations of danger have been well defined by Strachey in his summary of Freud's theories of anxiety:

The essence of a [traumatic situation] is an experience of helplessness . . . in the face of an accumulation of excitation, whether of external or internal origin, which cannot be dealt with. Anxiety "as a signal" is the response of the ego to the threat of the occurrence of a traumatic situation. Such a threat constitutes a situation of danger. Internal dangers change with the period of life (*Standard Edition* 20:81).

As we have discussed in chapter 4, in our consideration of the model of the reflex arc, as early as 1895 Freud had postulated that psychic organization must develop from an initial, "primary" functional state in which there is direct discharge by means of hallucinatory wish-fulfillment, to a "secondary" state capable of inhibiting direct discharge. Reality testing must gradually be acquired; this occurs through the repetitive experience of unpleasure which follows resort to discharge through the hallucinatory route. This is the reason for Freud's statement that "unpleasure remains the only means of education."[3]

Freud did not complete his work on the sequential unfolding of typical dangers until three decades after his initial effort of the *Project*. In *Inhibitions, Symptoms, and Anxiety* (1926), he pointed to the genesis of the secondary process in relationship to the child's gradual development of attachment to a particular mothering person. With this "relatedness" to the person who has provided the "specific actions" (cf. 1895, p. 318) required to avoid overstimulation and helplessness, the original danger of the traumatic accumulation of excitation is, in typical circumstances, replaced by the danger of losing the relatedness to mother, the danger of separation:

the content of the danger . . . is displaced from the economic situation on to the condition which determined that situation, viz., the loss of the object. . . . This change . . . represents a transition from the automatic and involuntary fresh appearance of anxiety to the intentional reproduction of anxiety as a signal of danger (1926 [1925], p. 138).[4]

As we have shown on figure 1, the separation anxiety phase may be further subdivided. Freud pointed out that in its later stages "it is no longer a matter of feeling the want of or actually losing the object itself, but of losing the object's love" (ibid., p. 143).

In 1926 Freud did not call attention to the fact that separation from the mother may be traumatic even if overstimulation is avoided by the provision of an adequate caretaking person. Such a drastic change in the child's world may constitute a narcissistic trauma; consequently, the line of development of narcissism is required for proper elucidation of these circumstances.[5] Freud did link the later forms of typical danger to the earlier ones through the common denominator of the child's narcissism. In the phallic phase, it is the penis which possesses the highest degree of narcissistic value. As a result, the typical danger situation of this developmental stage is the threat of the loss of the penis, or castration anxiety.

The sequence we have described may also be stated in terms of corresponding developments in the realm of object relations. After the establishment of a stable cognitive differentiation between the infant's self and his primary object, the danger of overstimulation is succeeded by that of separation anxiety. The fear of object loss remains the typical danger situation as long as the object is primarily a required portion of the child's narcissistic world, that is, an archaic "self-object." This state of affairs comes to an end with the consolidation of a cohesive self, following which omnipotent control over the object is no longer needed much of the time. Hence separation anxiety ceases to be the crucial danger situation. Now the absence of the object provokes jealousy to a greater degree than it creates separation anxiety, and the resultant hostility is the source of the fear of punishment or retaliation (the dread of castration).

Ferenczi (1926) has called the resolution of the Oedipus complex the most important psychic experience of separation in the course of childhood development. The fact that it leads to the formation of the superego renders this process into one that decisively alters psychic functioning. It makes the child autonomously self-regulating; henceforth, primarily he no longer fears retaliation or punishment by others. The typical danger becomes that of moral anxiety. At this point, the cardinal importance of object relations in the interpersonal sense begins to recede and is replaced as the matter of primary psychic import by intrapsychic conflicts. After the consolidation of a repression barrier, moral anxiety is replaced as the typical danger situation by that of realistic threats. The formation of this new structure constitutes the definitive differentiation of the ego from the id. At the same time, anxiety characteristically is brought into the service of the ego as a *signal* of danger.

The sequence of dangers as they have been outlined—overstimulation, object loss, castration, intrapsychic conflict, and realistic threats—may be divided into three successive time periods, each of which requires the utilization of a different model of the mind for its optimal understanding. The era of potential traumatic overstimulation calls for the use of the reflex arc model. From that nodal point in development when secure cognitive differentiation of the self from the object is achieved, the most applicable model is one based on the vicissitudes of the formation of self and objects in the representational world. When the formation of the superego ends the requirement for the participation of an outside person in the child's self-regulation, the self-object model ceases to be the most relevant one for the clarification of behavior. Through the phases in which intrapsychic conflicts succeed separation or castration anxieties as the typical dangers, the tripartite and topographic models are most applicable.

Freud was most careful to specify that each danger situation persists even after it has been succeeded as the typical one by some new threat:

I have had no intention of asserting that every later determinant of anxiety completely invalidates the preceding one. It is true that, as the development of the ego goes on, the earlier danger situations tend to lose their force and to be set aside. . . . Nevertheless, all these danger situations and determinants of anxiety can persist side by side and cause the ego to react to them with anxiety at a period later than the appropriate one; or, again, several of them can come into operation at the same time (1926 [1925], pp. 141–42).

In order to indicate that each danger situation may recur even when it is no longer the typical one, we have drawn a model in which the various developmental stages are indicated successively. In each stage, we have repeated the potential occurrence of every previous danger situation (see fig. 7).[6] This graphic device is intended to show that dangers are never completely left behind; rather, new ones are added. The same principle will apply to the other functions which the model will attempt to deal with, all of which will be represented through a similar series of layerings.

The diagram showing the hierarchy of danger situations typical for various developmental phases is in all ways characteristic for the model we shall develop in this monograph. This will consist of the superimposition of similar diagrams for a whole gamut of parallel developmental lines which must be studied in order to understand human behavior in depth. The resulting graphs show segments of development within which a particular function is performed in one specific way. At some nodal point, such as the formation of the superego, certain alterations in other functions permit or even necessitate a decisive shift, so that the function in question is henceforth carried out in a new manner. Under

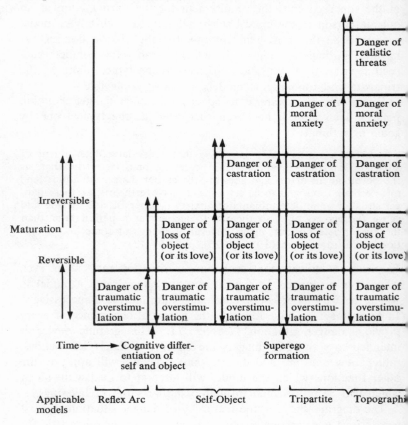

Fig. 7. The hierarchy of danger situations typical in various developmental phases.

certain conditions, however, the earlier, recently abandoned characteristics may once more come to the fore.

Various developmental lines may be superimposed only if each of them is subdivided into segments starting and ending at identical nodal points. Each of these turning points in development consists in the attainment of secondary autonomy for some "apparatus" of unusual importance—some internalization of structure that, in expectable circumstances, will no longer be subject to regressive dedifferentiation. On the diagrams, such changes will be indicated by a reversal in direction of one of the arrows, which originally run in opposite directions; when the arrows indicating maturation run in the same direction, structuralization has become irreversible.

CONSIDERATION OF ADDITIONAL DEVELOPMENTAL LINES: NARCISSISM, THE SENSE OF REALITY, TYPICAL DEFENSES

At this time we shall elaborate the model of developmental lines in interaction through the addition of three further functional hierarchies. Two of these have already been identified as prerequisites for the understanding of the development of anxiety and object relations: the developmental lines of narcissism and of the sense of reality. In fact, we have had to make certain preliminary statements about them in our presentation of the two hierarchies we have thus far discussed. The last function we shall include in this skeletal version of the model will be that of the defensive operations typical for each developmental phase.

Narcissism

The theoretical concept of narcissism was introduced by Freud in 1914. In accord with the general predominance of drive psychology in his theories of that era, Freud postulated that, upon achieving the capacity to differentiate cognitively between his own self and the object, the infant makes the crucial developmental step of distributing his libido into types: narcissistic and object libido. By choosing these terms, Freud was attempting to indicate that, depending on where they are invested, qualitative differences come into existence in various drive components.[7]

Freud went on to discuss the fate of "primary narcissism" in the later course of development:

Observation of normal adults shows that their former megalomania has been damped down and that the psychical characteristics from which we inferred their infantile narcissism have been effaced (1914, p. 93).

Such a person "has set up an *ideal* in himself by which he measures his actual [self]." This "ego ideal" constitutes "the target of the self-love which was enjoyed in childhood by the actual [self]" in those individuals whose development reaches expectable adult levels. As with his exposition of mental functioning in general, so in this matter Freud did not bother to fill in the intermediate steps between the initial conditions along this developmental line and those characteristic of its most mature evolution. Over the years, many psychoanalytic authors have contributed to the clinical understanding of these issues (cf. Nagera 1964; Federn 1926–52; A. Reich 1960). The metapsychological clarification necessary has only recently been made, however, through the work of Kohut (1966, 1968, 1971).

Kohut has made three principal contributions to a reformulation of the psychoanalytic theory of narcissism. The most fundamental of these has been that narcissism has a line of development separate from that of object libido. This implies that Freud's analogy about the investment of libido—that it is extended to and withdrawn from objects like the pseudopodia of an amoeba—is invalid. Kohut contradicts the concept that the investment of libido in an object diminishes the quantity of libido available for the self—or vice versa (cf. 1966).

The second of Kohut's theoretical innovations has been the conceptualization of two way-stations along the independent line of narcissistic development. These advances from primary narcissism have been designated as the "grandiose self" and the "idealized parent imago." The grandiose self refers to the infantile psyche in the stage Freud called the "purified pleasure ego," when it assigns all perfection to itself. It is therefore the dynamic source of personal ambitions, "closely interwoven with the drives and their inexorable tensions . . . [it] wants to be looked at and admired." In this stage, then, "narcissistic cathexis . . . is retained within the nexus of the self." In contrast, the idealized parental imago refers to an archaic "other"; it is therefore invested with narcissistic cathexis which is "amalgamated with features of true object love." Consequently, its appearance marks a phase-appropriate maturational step in the development of narcissistic libido. Subsequently, under the impact of object loss, frustration, or disappointment, identification with the idealized parent will take place. The greatest of these losses is that of Oedipal disappointment; this results in the internalization which eventuates in the formation of the superego:

The ego ideal is that aspect of the superego which corresponds to the phase-specific, massive introjection of the idealized qualities of the object (1966, p. 249).

Analogously, the grandiose self should undergo gradual modification,

merge with the structure of the ego's goals, and achieve autonomy. . . . The exhibitionism of the child must gradually become desexualized and subordinated to his goal-directed activities (p. 253).

The ideational content of the primitive exhibitionistic-narcissistic images of the grandiose self is the grandiose fantasy.

Kohut's third theoretical contribution on narcissism takes into account the transformations of primitive narcissism into functional attributes possessing secondary autonomy, such as wisdom, empathy, humor, creativity, and the acceptance of transience. These transformations follow upon the secure establishment of workable guiding ideals. On the hierarchical diagram we are proposing, considerations of this type are to be depicted as upward progress along the vertical axis.

The correlation of the development of narcissism with that of object love was begun by Freud in his 1914 discussion of the castration complex. He clarified that the preponderance of this constellation during one developmental phase, which at a later time (1923e) he was to name the "phallic phase," is based on the simultaneous maturation of object libido and the narcissistic cathexis of the phallus. The essential role of the castration complex in the resolution of the Oedipal libidinal and aggressive conflicts is a familiar aspect of Freud's psychology of development (cf. 1924d). Perhaps it has been less widely understood that Freud regarded the threat of castration specifically as a danger of *narcissistic* injury (cf. 1923e, 1925). Another way to state this would be that the gradual reduction of the child's grandiosity comes to include his phallus last of all, so that phallic exhibitionism, as well as its counterparts in females, continues to be subject to the excessive vulnerability that characterizes every aspect of the grandiose self. As Freud has pointed out (1919), whenever the Oedipus complex is poorly resolved, the consequence is a subjective sense of inferiority which can best be understood as a "narcissistic scar." In this particular perspective, it becomes evident that a prerequisite for the resolution of the Oedipus complex is sufficient maturation along the paths of transformation of narcissism to permit the child to tolerate the mortification caused by the collapse of his phallic grandiosity. This is not to be construed as the sole prerequisite for the resolution of the Oedipus complex, of course; to mention only the most essential requirements in terms of object love, the Oedipal object must have been cathected with sufficient intensity as a separate person and the entire Oedipal triad must have become the dominant ideational component of mental life.[8]

This may be the proper place to comment on the differences between male and female development with regard to these issues.[9] Freud (1925) concluded that a girl's awareness of her lack of a penis is a narcissistic injury which gives rise to a sense of inferiority and a "masculinity complex." Favorable feminine development depends on the acceptance of this narcissistic humiliation and, under the impact of the concurrent love for the father and rivalry with the mother, transformation of the wish for a penis into desire for a baby. Because the dissolution of the Oedipal complex in girls thus depends on libidinal frustration (instead of danger of castration, which is its prime causative agent in boys), the superego of women tends to function in a manner different from that of men (cf. Freud 1931b). These differences between the development of men and women, however, do not significantly affect the applicability of the same model of the mind to both.

We may now be ready to integrate the developmental line of narcissism with the model drawn to illustrate those of object relations and the typical situations of danger. It will be recalled that in the diagram (fig. 7) no attempt had been made to account for the transition from the situation in which the predominant danger is that of separation to the one in which castration is the typical threat. The gradual reduction in the scope of the grandiose self which we have outlined in considering the line of development of narcissism now permits us to explain this transition: it occurs whenever the scope of grandiosity becomes irreversibly confined to the child's phallus. Similarly, the idealization of the parents then becomes focused on their phallic attributes.

We must now superimpose the line of development of narcissism on figure 7. When this is done, it will be seen that, prior to cognitive differentiation of self from the object, a state of primary narcissism prevails. Following the achievement of cognitive self-object differentiation, the era of separation anxiety corresponds to that of the grandiose self and idealized parental imagoes. When narcissistic grandiosity becomes confined to the phallus, castration anxiety gradually displaces the threat of loss of the archaic self-object as the typical danger. Superego formation entails the internalization of the ego ideal as well as a shift to the preponderance of intersystemic conflicts, that is, the emergence of moral anxiety as the typical danger. After the consolidation of the repression barrier, these conflicts are no longer directly discernible; anxiety is typically confined to its function as a signal of danger, and narcissism ordinarily takes the form of its matured transformations into empathy, creativity, wisdom, and humor. These relationships are graphically portrayed in figure 8.

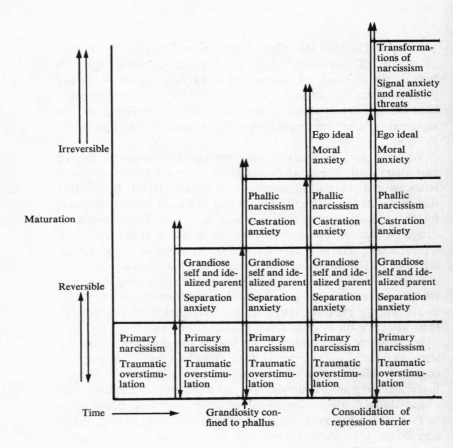

Fig. 8. The hierarchies of narcissism and danger situations
      typical in various phases of object relations.

The Sense of Reality

In *Formulations on the Two Principles of Mental Functioning,*
Freud had left open the related questions of the mode of development of secondary process thinking and the acceptance of the
reality principle from the preceding primary states—primary
process thought and the pleasure principle. The attempt to fill

the way-stations between the "primary psychical stage" and the "secondary stage" characteristic of the normal adult in waking thought fell to Ferenczi (1913). In doing this he constructed the first psychoanalytic line of development,[10] which can be correlated with Piaget's later and more elaborate description of cognitive development in the child (cf. Piaget and Inhelder 1966).

Ferenczi began his exposition with Freud's finding in the case of the Rat Man (1909d) that in obsessional neurosis the patient is convinced of the omnipotence of his thoughts. Ferenczi carefully described what was later to be called "splitting of the ego" in these patients. One portion of their psychic organization remains developmentally arrested in the stage of magical thinking, while another, having reached acceptance of the reality principle, is able to view the primitive thinking of the other fragment of the personality as ludicrous. Ferenczi interpreted the primitive thinking as a regression to the stage of childhood development characterized by a lack of impulse control. Freud had related the fantasy of omnipotence to the megalomania of infancy; it corresponds to the era of the grandiose self on our diagrams.

According to Ferenczi,

the replacement of childhood megalomania by the recognition of the power of natural forces composes the essential content of the development of the ego (p. 218).

We assume that here Ferenczi was referring to the establishment of a stable representation of the self. (We prefer to use the designation "self system" in such a context.) [11] Ferenczi conceived of childhood megalomania as the persistence of a stage of "unconditional omnipotence" which immediately follows intrauterine existence. Although the term "primary narcissism" was not to be introduced until the following year, Ferenczi must have had in mind that such a stage cannot long prevail, in spite of the best efforts of the mothering persons. Frustrations must inevitably interfere with the illusion of unconditional omnipotence. Whenever nurture is successful in satisfying the infant's wishes, however, "he must feel himself in the possession of a magical capacity that can actually realize all his wishes." Ferenczi named this era "the period of magic hallucinatory omnipotence." He argued that normal adults return to this stage of organization in the state of sleep and dreaming and that psychoses constitute "the pathological counterpart of this regression."[12]

In order to improve the frequency with which the nurturing persons may be able to satisfy his wishes, the child has to learn to give signals by means of motoric activities. At first, whenever they happen to be followed by gratification, the infant will experience his uncoordinated motor discharges as if they constituted magical signals. Later, a specialized gesture language is developed for this purpose. Consequently, Ferenczi named the next stage the "period of omnipotence by the help of magic gestures." It is paralleled in adult life by the use of various magical rituals.

The failure of these magical measures to bring about real satisfaction eventually causes the collapse of the illusion of omnipotence. It is through this confrontation with his inability to control magically the external world that the infant gradually learns to make the cognitive distinction between the outside and his own self. This achievement brings to an end the era of primary narcissism and inaugurates that of the idealized parental imagoes. Ferenczi assumed that the child next goes through an animistic period in which "every object appears to him to be endowed with life." This implies that objects are seen only as projected or mirrored representations of the self, although cognitively they are already recognized as external to it.[13] The nurturing figures, now endowed with magical powers, may respond to the child's wishes even at this stage—provided that he learns "to represent an object symbolically." Consequently, Ferenczi stated that "if the child is surrounded by loving care, he need not . . . give up the illusion of his omnipotence" (1913, pp. 228–29). Naturally, much the most important means of symbolic communication is that of speech. Its greater effectiveness promotes the gradual replacement of gesture symbolism by a "period of magic thoughts and magic words." This is the stage reproduced in adulthood in obsessional neuroses as well as in certain religious beliefs and practices (cf. Freud 1913 [1912–13]).

According to Ferenczi,

Freud dates the end of the domination of the pleasure principle only from the complete psychical detachment from the parents (1913, p. 232).

Although we can find no specific published statement by Freud to this effect, we believe it to be an accurate summation of his theoretical position.[14]

The era in which behavior is typically regulated by the reality principle is not securely established until after the resolution of the Oedipus complex. Ferenczi showed that the feeling of omnipotence persists longer in the realm of sexuality than in other areas of life. He explained this on the grounds that the possibility of "autoerotic" gratification prolongs the sway of the pleasure principle in this sector of behavior. (In this context, it might have been preferable to use the term "libidinal self-satisfaction" to designate the results of masturbation in view of the fact that Freud had used the word "autoerotism" to designate the earliest stage of libidinal development, that preceding narcissism.) We have already made this same distinction in tracing the developmental line of narcissism by noting that grandiosity about the phallus is the last aspect of infantile megalomania to be given up.

After the acceptance of the reality principle, man's need for omnipotence may find waking expression only in his artistic products which partake of consciously shared illusions. It might be reemphasized here that the surrender of infantile omnipotence under the impact of the frustrations of reality, such as those of the oedipal defeat, contributes to the consolidation of the self as a psychic system. It provides an increasingly more accurate definition of the actual limits and capabilities of the self, thus ending the possibility of permanent splits in the self (in expectable circumstances) once the omnipotent illusions of the sexual sphere are given up.

The Typical Mechanisms of Defense

The last of the developmental lines to be presented in this chapter is that of the hierarchy of the typical mechanisms of defense. The graphic representation of this line, as well as that of the development of the sense of reality, appears in figure 9.

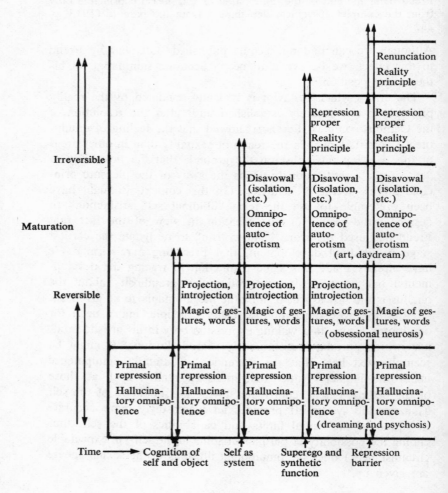

Fig. 9. A hierarchical model of the developmental lines of the sense of reality and the typical defensive operations.

Freud had conceptualized psychic defenses in the early 1890s on the basis of clinical observations of various neuroses in which unpleasurable ideas or affects had been actively warded off.[15] He described a series of methods of defense in these differing neurotic syndromes (1894, 1896). He emphasized the fact that defenses operate unconsciously, and specified in detail the operation of repression, isolation of affect, reaction formation, and projection.

As Anna Freud has pointed out (1965), these important distinctions, spelled out in Freud's early papers, were temporarily lost sight of during the period Freud devoted to the exploration of the unconscious. From about 1900 to 1926, the term "repression" was used almost interchangeably with "defense."[16] In *Inhibitions, Symptoms, and Anxiety*, Freud once more stated that the concept of defense would be employed

as a general designation for all the techniques which the ego makes use of in conflicts which may lead to neurosis (p. 163).

(The "ego" was here being designated in terms of the structural theory as one set of enduring mental functions.)

As typical methods of defense, Freud differentiated the use of repression in hysteria from the uses of regression of the libido, reaction formation, isolation of affect, and undoing in obsessional neurosis. Taking a developmental point of view, he also stated:

It may well be that before its sharp cleavage into an ego and an id, and before the formation of a superego, the mental apparatus makes use of different methods of defense from those which it employs after it has reached these stages of organization (ibid., p. 164).

In her 1936 monograph, Anna Freud enumerated various early defenses which had been described in the course of Freud's work. She listed introjection and projection, reversal into the opposite, turning against the self, and displacement of instinctual aims. She then attempted to arrange the defenses into a developmental sequence:

Projection and introjection were methods which depended on the differentiation of the ego [self?] from the outside world. The expulsion of ideas or affects from the ego [self?] and their relegation to the outside world would be a relief to the ego [self?] only when it had learnt to distinguish itself from that world" (p. 55 [our interpolations]). "Such processes as regression, reversal, and turning round upon the self are probably . . . as old as the instincts themselves, or at least as old as the conflict between instinctual impulses and any hindrance which they may encounter on their way to gratification (p. 56).

In other words, these instinctual vicissitudes develop gradually during the era in which the mental apparatus still functions on the model of the reflex arc. The mechanisms of projection and introjection can be added to the defensive repertoire only after the irreversible establishment of cognitive differentiation between the self and the object.[17]

Anna Freud also examined the most mature end of this developmental line, pointing out that the displacements of sexual aim which constitute the possibility of sublimation are based on the prior knowledge and acceptance of "higher social values." In other words, sublimation cannot be utilized until after the formation of the superego. As Anna Freud stated,

the defense mechanisms of repression and sublimation could not be employed until relatively late in the process of development (1936, p. 56).

She did not provide a specific rationale, however, for the late acquisition of these capacities. Elaboration of a hierarchical model may explain and buttress these conclusions (see also Hartmann 1950b, pp. 124–26).

At any rate, sublimation and repression as defenses clearly belong to the era following Oedipal resolution. On our diagrams, we have indicated that the establishment of the repression barrier can only take place after this resolution is completed. Here we wish to highlight Anna Freud's insistence that "it is meaningless to speak of repression where the ego is still merged with the id." We have already quoted Freud's statement of 1926 that the "sharp cleavage into an ego and an id"—a condition which we assume to imply relative irreversibility in this respect—is associated with the formation of the superego.[18] More recently, views have been put forward concerning the differentiation of the ego from the common matrix it shares with the id at a much earlier point. A more detailed discussion of ego development is therefore necessary to resolve these differing points of view.

In chapter 1 we reviewed the evolution of Freud's concept of the ego and concluded that he had not concerned himself to any appreciable extent with the problem of its development. The first extensive discussion of this issue was that of Hartmann, Kris, and Loewenstein (1946):

> During the undifferentiated phase there is maturation of apparatuses that later will come under the control of the ego, and that serve motility, perception, and certain thought processes. Maturation in these areas proceeds without the total organization we call ego; only after ego formation will these functions be fully integrated (p. 36).

It is essential to grasp that the conceptualization of an undifferentiated phase and of apparatuses of primary autonomy did not lead these authors to postulate that ego formation is accomplished as soon as the capacity to distinguish self from nonself is acquired. They stressed that this ability is only the first, albeit the most fundamental, of the steps which lead to the formation of the ego. It is followed by the gradual development of the capacity to postpone gratification, which probably takes place through identification with the nursing mother as well as through the maturation of further apparatuses. The limitations of reality thus become accepted in time.

The formation of the ego proceeds best in situations of optimal frustration:

> in order to retain the love of his environment, the child learns to control his instinctual drives; this means that the differentiation between the id and ego becomes ever more complete as the child grows (ibid., p. 45).
> . . . with the existence of repression the demarcation between id and ego is drawn more sharply and maintained by countercathexes (ibid., p. 46).

Hartmann, Kris, and Loewenstein thus took the position that the definitive differentiation between the ego and the id can only take place when, under the impact of castration anxiety, the child learns to control his phallic libido and aggression. Consequently, the irreversible establishment of the ego cannot be expected to take place until after the resolution of the Oedipus complex. The same implication can be drawn from an observation reported by Freud in many of his early writings (1899, 1901, 1905): namely, the fact that infantile amnesia generally extends through the sixth or the eighth year of life. From this clinical generalization it may be inferred that repression as the prime mode of defense does not begin until around that age. We are defining the demarcation of the ego from the id in terms of the advent of repression as the typical, albeit never as the sole, mechanism of defense.

With this discussion of ego formation, we can return to the topic of the developmental line of the defenses. It must be emphasized once again that each mechanism occupies the role of typical or predominant mode of defense only for a particular span of the course of development, although the fact that a given defense mechanism is predominant does not mean that other defenses are not utilized within that phase of development. Once a defense mechanism is acquired as a functional capacity, it can always be called upon in case of need. In addition, the concept of typical defenses does not imply that the mental mechanisms in question arise de novo at the inception of the particular phase in which they come to serve the typical defensive function. On the contrary, each mechanism must have an earlier history, a period of genesis in the course of which it does not serve the defensive function as yet.[19]

After it has been succeeded as the characteristic mode of defense, every mechanism may undergo a change of function so that it may begin to operate in the service of nondefensive, adaptive tasks. Concurrently, in case of greater than expectable stress, regression may occur to the earlier mode of organization, once more reinstating the defensive function of the mechanism.[20] Finally, the hierarchy of defenses we are about to propose is arranged in the sequence in which these mechanisms are utilized as the typical ones; this is not to be confused with the sequence of their genesis as mental processes, which may be quite different.

As we have seen, Anna Freud (1936) arranged the defenses into a developmental line and placed instinctual vicissitudes at the earliest stage of this sequence. Glover (1950) expressed agreement with this point of view. He added that the next phase can be conceptualized as the setting up of a system of anticathexis. He stressed that this system is, to begin with, one of response to traumatic stress rather than to internal conflict. The principal anticathectic process is that of primal repression. Strictly speaking, such a mechanism is not a defensive operation but, rather, a consequence of the incapacity actively to erect defenses; the primal repression is passively experienced and unavoidable.

In his paper on repression (1915d), Freud had made the assumption that, before the establishment of "repression proper," there is a phase of

primal repression . . . which consists in the psychical (ideational) representative of the instinct being denied entrance into the conscious (p. 148).

The history of the concept of primal repression has been ably reviewed by Frank and Muslin (1967). They have pointed out that Freud (1915e) had assumed that an anticathexis must be set up in order to maintain a primal repression; with repression proper, "there is in addition withdrawal of the *Pcs.* cathexis." In 1926, Freud raised the possibility that it is after the formation of the superego that repression proper replaces primal repression. This suggestion implies that, after the achievement of autonomy in self-regulation, the derivatives of dangerous impulses must be permanently excluded from awareness. Prior to such autonomy, it is only necessary to conceal these ideas from others; only those conditions which cause actual unpleasure, that is, trauma, have to be warded off, so that the operation of primal repression suffices. To be sure, we would expect the transition from the earlier stage to the later one to take place somewhat gradually.

As we have noted in our discussion of the topographic theory, primal repression is that automatic avoidance of the unpleasurable which is characteristic of the primary mental processes. Therefore, although it may not be available as early in life as are the instinctual vicissitudes, it is primal repression that must be considered as the "typical" mechanism of defense of the phase of mental function on the model of the reflex arc: it is the first mental mechanism which possesses an adaptive purpose. Although primal repression continues to be the defense which becomes operative in case of traumatic overstimulation throughout the life span, the era in which such contingencies are most likely to arise is that of early infancy. With expectable maturation and psychic development, this era is soon succeeded by one in which defenses have to be erected against intrapsychic conflicts, in addition to the former measures which ward off overstimulation. This progression parallels the acquisition of the capacity to differentiate the self from the external world cognitively.

Anna Freud's view that the achievement of differentiation makes it possible to begin to utilize the mechanisms of projection and introjection for defensive purposes has already been cited. We should like to underscore once again that this is not the starting point for the occurrence of these mental processes; they exist as processes without defensive aims at an earlier stage of infancy. They occupy the position of *typical* defenses during a limited period of development, that phase which lies between the acquisition of the capacity to differentiate cognitively the self from the nonself and the consolidation of reality testing. The necessary correlation between the achievement of reality testing and the coalescence of the self as a stable system has already been described by Modell (1968). This coalescence implies that henceforth it is not possible to avoid acknowledging even those aspects of the self which are experienced as narcissistically unpleasurable or dangerous from the point of view of libido or aggression; thus the reality of one's own qualities becomes more stably perceived, with a concomitant improvement in one's grasp of the realities of the external world.

Projection as the typical mode of defense corresponds to the preoedipal phobias of young children, to their fears of external objects or noises which can serve as representations of their own dangerous internal excitements. The projective mechanisms seen in the psychoses have a similar significance. These instances should be differentiated from the more mature projections seen in the neuroses, conditions which occur after a repression barrier has already been established. In the characteristic zoophobias of the "infantile neurosis" which occurs after the formation of the superego, as well as in the phobias of adults, there are projective mechanisms. These are much more limited in significance, however, than are the massive projections of the young child; moreover, projection is not the typical defense in these later conditions. In a sense, projection also continues to mature as a mechanism; with the refinement of the capacity to perceive reality, it comes to underlie the developed empathic capacities of adults.

Rapaport (1967 [1944]) has described the varied uses of projection in a similar developmental sequence. It should be kept in mind that the possibility of using this mechanism depends on the capacity to distinguish the self from the object. What have been called "projections" of psychotics are often caused by failure to maintain this boundary of the self; the attribution of a thought or feeling of one's own to another is due to the lack of differentiation between self and object. Similarly, even some later preoedipal "projections" are more properly explained as "externalizations," when some unbearable impulse is merely cast out from the self and not necessarily assigned to a particular object. As Jacobson (1964) noted, "projection" and "introjection" are terms which have been utilized with insufficient precision in the literature; these confusions can be avoided if each behavior is assessed in terms of the hierarchy of developmental possibilities.

Once the self becomes defined as a psychic unit in accord with the actualities, it becomes impossible to use the attribution of dangerous impulses to others as the typical mode of defense. From this time on and until the internalization of moral standards, the typical defense is the disavowal of dangerous realities. The internalization of morality terminates this state of affairs by necessitating the setting up of permanent countercathexes in order to keep unacceptable mental contents in repression. We must review Freud's thoughts about the problem of the perception of external reality for a proper elucidation of the mechanism of disavowal.

Basch (1968) has shown that Freud's best effort to conceptualize the probem of external perception was made in the *Project for a Scientific Psychology*, especially as modified in letter 39 to Wilhelm Fliess (Freud 1950a). Here Freud first postulated a mental apparatus with separate perceptual and memory systems. He elaborated a crucial hypothesis, confirmed by much research on perception since that time (cf. G. Klein 1959), to the effect that the perceptual system, designated as *phi*, invariably transmits the stimuli it receives to consciousness. The latter was defined as an intermediate agency, called *omega*, which imparted sensory qualities to the percepts. These sensory qualities may then be noted by the memory system, which was termed *psi*; this step in the process depends on the employment of attention cathexis. At the inception of mental life, there is no capacity to select those perceptions which are to be registered in memory: even those which give rise to unpleasure are cathected.[21] Consequently, Freud postulated that there is a need to develop some defense mechanism which will enable the child rapidly to decathect unpleasurable perceptions. The decathexis of endogenous stimuli which produce unpleasure is the mechanism of primary repression. Prior to the formation of the superego, however, most threats of traumatization involve real events in the interpersonal field, so that primary repression is by itself insufficient as a defense against unpleasurable perceptions. Basch points out that Freud was not to solve the problem of defense against unavoidable external perceptions until he described the mechanism of disavowal in the 1920s.

Freud began his use of the concept of disavowal in 1923, in a series of papers dealing with the phallic phase of psychosexual development. He reported the observation that children will disavow the significance of their accurate perception of the absence of a penis in the female (see also Freud 1924c, 1925). In the paper on *Fetishism* (1927), he stressed that the correct perception persists in the memory system, yet the belief in the phallic woman is also retained. He noted that the mechanism was also observable in instances where some other unpleasurable external perception has to be defended against.[22]

Freud called the consequences of disavowal a "splitting of the ego." When he returned to this theme (1940 [1938]), he stressed that children are often confronted with the choice between instinctual renunciation and the disavowal of reality. Disavowal involves a "rift in the ego," an abandonment of its synthetic function. In one fragment of the personality, behavior is based on the acknowledgment of the real state of affairs, in another on its disregard. In his last statement, in the *Outline* (1940a [1938]), Freud spelled out that disavowal of external percepts takes place during the same period of childhood in which instinctual demands are warded off through repressions.[23]

Once again, we must emphasize that disavowal is the typical defense for this limited developmental span but has a nondefensive prehistory in the era of disparate self-nuclei, before the secure establishment of a unitary, cohesive self. The phase of disavowal as typical defense is concluded once the synthetic function has matured sufficiently to make any regressive fragmentation of the cohesive self impossible under expectable circumstances. This achievement increases castration anxiety by making the defenses less effective, and thereby promotes the eventual resolution of the Oedipus complex. The concomitant formation of the superego renders it no longer sufficient merely to keep dangerous ideas to oneself: thenceforth such ideas must be banished from consciousness through repression proper.

Repression is the defense typical for the era of the infantile neurosis—that of intrapsychic conflicts of the ego with both superego and drives. Repression proper implies the setting up of permanent countercathexes. This is another way of stating that a repression barrier has been erected or structuralized. This is the developmental step usually referred to as the consolidation of the system Ego. Once the repression barrier has become immune to regressive deactivation in expectable circumstances, or once the child can no longer experience incestuous, cannibalistic, or other primitive impulses as such, novel dangers from the drives will be dealt with through renunciation, without defensive efforts. We have dealt with but a fraction of the repertoire of defenses described in current clinical theory, those we have deemed to be *typical* at various phases of psychic development. A similar point of view is implicit in the work of Rapaport (cf. 1961 [1953]). The task of fitting the remaining defenses into the schema cannot be attempted at this time. To illustrate how this can be done, however, we can point to the probability that isolation of affect might be based on processes similar to those underlying disavowal, and might thus belong, characteristically, to the same stage of psychic organization (see also Gedo, in Abrams 1971).[24]

The superimposition of various developmental lines produces a hierarchical model of the development of the structure of the mind. We should like to reserve discussion of this complex model and its comparison to other models of the mind for the next chapter.

7 The Hierarchy of Modes of Psychic Functioning

In order to arrange the various modes or systems of psychic functioning considered in psychoanalysis into an overall hierarchical schema, we have attempted to review what we consider to be the optimal explanatory range of each analytic model of the mind. We approached this task by summarizing the specific observational data that had led Freud to the construction of each model, and we illustrated the utilization of each model in organizing clinical data by citing some of Freud's best-known case histories.

Each of the models of psychoanalytic theory we have dealt with appears to depict separate subsystems of mental functioning, each at a different maturational phase along the scale of the progressive differentiation of the entire psyche. The subsystems may be fitted together into a supraordinate hierarchical model through detailed examination of certain relevant lines of development.

No discussion of hierarchical or supraordinate conceptualizations of human development can be adequate without reference to the work of Erik Erikson (1959). His careful and detailed description of the human life cycle need not be reviewed here. We emphasize, however, that Erikson's work directs attention to the human being within the social world. As he stated in *Young Man Luther* (1958):

We cannot even begin to encompass a human being without indicating for each of the stages of his life cycle the framework of social influences and of traditional institutions which determine his perspectives in his more infantile past and in his more adult future (p. 20).

Our effort to develop a hierarchical model will not attempt to satisfy such a requirement. We feel that the psychoanalytic method is an observational tool which produces a unique body of data in a particular universe of discourse. When we step outside of the psychoanalytic situation, we enter another universe of discourse; hence it is difficult to correlate psychoanalytic propositions with those collected within the social field, or, for that matter, with those of brain physiology. Bridging attempts which try to encompass both psychoanalysis and one of these neighboring fields may be doomed to failure; they may even do a disservice by confusing the issues (cf. Rosenblueth 1971). The scientific problem of different levels of observation is better handled through the systems approach, as we have indicated in chapter 1. Although we have confined our attention to the interacting systems of the psyche as they may be observed through the psychoanalytic treatment procedure, we do not find any inconsistency between our concepts and those of Erikson, which deal with a different order of interacting systems.

A brief review of the argument contained in the preceding chapters may help to clarify our conceptualization of the hierarchical model. Freud proposed the topographic model for the purpose of explicating the psychology of dreams (1900). He found this could be done by postulating the existence of two psychic systems, the *Pcs.* and the *Ucs.* The contents of the former are accessible to consciousness through increased attention cathexis; the latter's contents can only become conscious by way of the formation of transferences onto *Pcs.* elements. Freud applied this conceptualization only to the functional state of adults; in the case of children's dreams, he found no division or censorship between *Pcs.* and *Ucs.* Psychoneurotic symptoms, like dreams, were seen as compromise formations that transferred the primary process characteristics of the *Ucs.* onto *Pcs.* processes.

Freud later encountered other clinical phenomena, such as negative therapeutic reactions, that did not fit into the topographic model. In 1923, he grouped sets of mental functions in accord with new criteria, unrelated to accessibility to consciousness, to produce a second psychoanalytic model of the mind. That organization of mental processes which controls motility, which produces resistances, and which concerns itself with adaptation, was defined as the ego. The part of the mind which consists of drive pressures was conceived of as the id. Ideals and the moral sense, which, like the defenses, are primarily unconscious, were placed in a separate agency, the superego. The model consisting of these three functional sets is the tripartite model. Freud compared the relation between the ego and the id to the one between a rider and his horse: the ego controls the drives but never absolutely; the balance between these forces must always be determined in accord with the demands of the superego as well as those of external reality. In other words, the tripartite model portrays behaviors that result from intrapsychic conflicts.

We have spotlighted the desirability of developing additional theoretical tools for the study of mental functioning at those stages of development that precede superego formation. In his studies of early stages of mental life, Freud himself turned to the problems of the self and its objects in the examination of narcissism (1914). He thus distinguished a group of "narcissistic neuroses" from the "transference neuroses" which he had elucidated using the topographic model. In the narcissistic neuroses, presumably organized in the mode of the earlier stages of development, frustration led to increased investment of libido in the self. In contrast, in the transference neuroses, frustration led to the cathexis of object representations or fantasies. Our view is that the vicissitudes of relations between the self and objects preceding superego formation are so paramount for the understanding of mental functioning that one must construct explicit models of the mind to elucidate these particular modes of psychic organization.[1]

Even this mode of organization is a result of prior developmental achievements. At the start of psychic life, the self is not yet distinguished or separated from the object. The process of this earliest psychic development has been described only by recent psychoanalytic research. However, Freud had already proposed a distinct model applicable to the conditions he hypothesized for the starting point of mental life. This is the reflex arc model of 1900. Freud understood the crucial function of the mental apparatus at the stage before self-object differentiation to be that of avoidance of overstimulation. These psychoeconomic considerations have been adequate for the explanation of hallucinatory phenomena and other states of immediate tension discharge.

In the past thirty years, psychoanalytic psychology has expanded beyond these subsystems to include within its scope the study of nonpathological, conflict-free personality functions (cf. Hartmann 1939). The introduction of these new aspects of theory into the construction of models of the mind was initiated by Kohut and Seitz (1963). They wrote:

> in the structural model of the psyche, the barrier of defenses separates only a small part of the infantile psychological depth from the areas of mature functioning, while the deep, unconscious activities in the remainder of the diagram are in broad uninterrupted contact with the preconscious layers of the surface. Kohut has referred to the dichotomized segment of the psyche as the area of transferences, and to the uninterrupted segment as the area of progressive neutralization (p. 136).

It is interesting to recall in this connection that in *The Unconscious* (1915), Freud had already made this kind of distinction between unconscious contents which can pass into consciousness and those which are repressed. This important modification of the theories embodied in the topographic model was further elaborated by Kohut and Seitz:

> infantile impulses, which have met with frustration of traumatic intensity, exert their transference influence across the barrier of defenses and produce compromise formations (between primary and secondary processes) with the preconscious contents of the ego. . . . the infantile impulses which have encountered optimal frustration are transformed gradually into neutralized mental activities (p. 137).

In other words, this model acknowledges that human mental life resembles not only the rider on his horse of Freud's analogy of 1923, but also, in a different set of circumstances—that is, in the absence of intrapsychic conflict—the image of a centaur: a creature combining the qualities of horse-ness and rider-ness in one entity. The model proposed by Kohut and Seitz is applicable only to the fully differentiated psyche, or to that stage of structuralization which is attained after the resolution of the Oedipus complex. Even for this restricted segment of mental life, these authors found it necessary to blend the topographic and the tripartite models in order to do justice to the range of observable phenomena. For an understanding of the full range of human potentialities, including the more archaic modes of mental functioning, it is essential, therefore, to construct a model encompassing everything Kohut and Seitz have considered, as well as those conditions portrayed by the reflex arc and self-object models.

It is with this purpose in mind that we are using the device of outlining a series of developmental lines. This approach introduces a consistent genetic viewpoint in the depiction of mental functioning by specifying the principal steps in the formation of mental structure. In so doing, we may be able to overcome the difficulty in correlating the diverse models of psychoanalytic theory outlined in the above discussion. These models were devised to clarify specific modes of functioning which appear to have no overt connecting links with each other but which can be shown to form subsystems of the overall hierarchy of the mind. The lines of development describe the evolution of various functions which are represented in each of the subsystems, and thus demonstrate the underlying connections among these (cf. Suslick, in Gedo and Goldberg 1970).

The developmental schema we have constructed cuts across the boundaries assumed by the previously proposed models of psychic functioning. If this schema is charted on a rectangular coordinate graph, similar to figures 1, 7, 8, and 9, we obtain a hierarchical model of mental functions (see fig. 10). Its horizontal axis may accommodate any set of lines of development deemed necessary for the understanding of whatever clinical data are under scrutiny. Because successively acquired functions do not replace each other but are added cumulatively to the repertoire of behavioral potentialities, mental life and its portrayal in this type of model become progressively more elaborate with maturation. In certain situations, regressions to more archaic modes of organization may occur, but functions that have attained autonomy from conflict may not participate in these returns to more primitive positions. This kind of irreversibility of function with maturation may be indicated along the vertical axis of the developmental model.

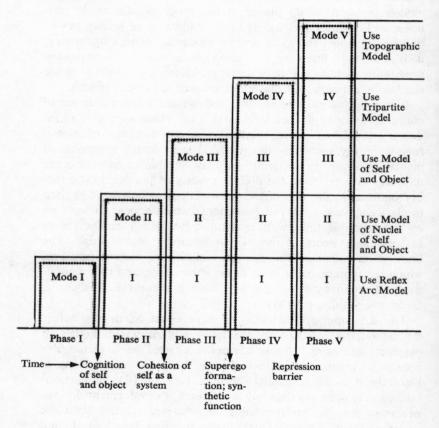

Fig. 10. The hierarchical model of subsystems of psychic functioning.

The lines of development we selected for extended discussion were those we have found to be essential for the differentiation of a minimal scheme of psychoanalytic nosology. This issue will be further elaborated in chapter 11. The selected lines fall into a series of parallel phases which are consistently separated from each other by the same nodal points of developmental transition (see fig. 10):

Phase I extends from birth until the acquisition of the capacity to distinguish cognitively the self from the object.

Phase II covers the span between this point and the functional separation of the self from the object, or the essentially irreversible unification of the self as a psychic entity. This marks the end of discrete, nonintegrated areas of mental functioning.

Phase III extends from the consolidation of the cohesive self to the formation of the superego.

Phase IV extends from superego formation to the completion of ego differentiation with the laying down of the repression barrier.

Phase V constitutes the era of the fully differentiated psychic apparatus.

This succession of phases constitutes a temporal record showing an epigenetic schema of expectable personality development. In addition, it serves simultaneously as an outline of a series of modes of personality organization, arranged in order of increasing complexity. Any one person may function in accord with any of these modes of organization at any given time. In order to make a "cross-sectional" assessment, that is, to decide how an individual is functioning at a particular moment, it is necessary to determine his status with regard to each of the functions referred to in the lines of development included in the schema. For a long-term evaluation of the ranges of a person's functional capacities, the model permits the charting of the progressive and regressive alterations in his mode of personality organization over time.

Because of the close interdependence of the various functions included in the model, it is to be expected that ordinarily each individual would be characterized by being in the same developmental phase for each of these developmental lines. This implies that all of these cardinal aspects of the mind would ordinarily form cohesive clusters. Those functions which have gained autonomy from conflicts will usually be spared whenever regressive movements in psychic organization take place; therefore, the autonomous functions would constitute exceptions to the prevailing organization of psychic life in terms of some specific developmental phase or cluster.

The five modes of functional organization which correspond to the various developmental phases portrayed by the model may be summarized as follows.

In Mode I, self and object are not differentiated; the typical danger is that of overstimulation; primary narcissism and unconditional omnipotence are in force; and the protodefensive mechanisms of primal repression or the occurrence of instinctual vicissitudes are characteristic.

In Mode II, the grandiose self is consistently distinguished from idealized parental imagoes; the typical danger is that of separation from these objects; omnipotent illusions are perpetuated through magic; and the mechanisms of projection and introjection are the typical defenses. This mode of organization is achieved with entry into Phase II and may be regressively reactivated in later phases.

In Mode III, infantile narcissism and omnipotent illusions have become confined to the sphere of sexuality; the typical danger is the threat of castration; the typical defense is that of disavowal; and both the self and the object have attained wholeness. This mode is reached with the start of Phase III and remains potentially available thereafter.

In Mode IV, mental life begins to follow the reality principle and is guided by the ego ideal; the typical danger is that of moral anxiety; and the typical defense is repression proper. This mode is available only in Phases IV and V.

In Mode V, anxiety is typically reduced to its signal function; drive pressures which might create dangers are handled through renunciation; narcissism takes the forms of wisdom, empathy, humor, and creativity; and the typical dangers are those inherent in external realities. These conditions obtain in Phase V only.

As we have indicated in figure 10, the reflex arc model is most suitable for the elucidation of behavior organized in Mode I; the self and object models are optimal for Modes II and III; and the tripartite and topographic models, or their combination in the manner suggested by Kohut and Seitz, are most appropriate to clarify the later modes of behavior.

Before the unification of the self and of the object at the conclusion of Phase II, mental function consists of discrete, separated aspects of activity between parts of the self and parts of objects. The nature of the nucleus of self and that of the part object involved in any one activity depends on the specific drive seeking discharge through the given activity. In adult life, regressions to this level of organization, that is, to Mode II, are seen in delusional states in which fragmentation of the self has occurred. The resultant chaotic aspects of the self may later be regrouped around one dominant psychic feature during the recovery phase. As Freud noted in his discussion of Schreber's illness (1911), several fixation points may be formed in the course of development; any one of these may or may not acquire pathological significance in the course of the person's life. In other words, the use of the model of nuclei of self and objects may be appropriate not only during that part of childhood we have here designated as Phase II and in the psychotic fragmentations of the self; it is also useful for the study of certain isolated behaviors of nonpsychotic adults.

Correspondingly, the model of the whole self and of whole objects becomes most appropriate as soon as these consolidations into cohesive, unitary entities have taken place, that is, when the child enters Phase III. Mode III is characteristic not only of this era of childhood, however, but also of certain psychopathological conditions and behaviors without pathological significance in adult life.

Distinctions similar to the ones just made for the use of the two kinds of models of self and objects may also be made between the optimal utilization of the tripartite and topographic models, respectively. In the era of the infantile neurosis, that of Phase IV, as well as in adult psychopathology which consists of a regression to similar conditions (those of Mode IV), the tripartite model serves to illuminate psychic functioning in a parsimonious manner. Conditions characterized by Mode V may occur with some rarity, so that this mode and the topographic model which best illustrates it are pertinent only for isolated behaviors such as parapraxes, jokes, successful dreams, and the like. Expectable functioning in adults is therefore best understood in practice by a combination of the topographic and tripartite models, such as the one proposed by Kohut and Seitz in 1963.

The hierarchical model is an oversimplified and arbitrary schema. One cannot draw legitimate deductions from its correlates in a rigid manner, as it is by no means complete.[2] In specific clinical contexts additional developmental lines must be considered; their use might well require subdivision of the hierarchy into a different set of phases, leading to the delimitation of new clusters or modes of functioning. The resultant modifications of the model would not require that the principles on which it has been constructed be called into question, however. Therefore we need not attempt to provide further elaborations of the model at this time.[3] In the chapters that follow we will provide a demonstration of the model's usefulness as it is applied to the manifold human activities that behavioral scientists are called upon to understand.

8 A Demonstration of the Clinical Utilization of the Hierarchical Model

In order to demonstrate the superior utility of the hierarchical model for the organization of clinical data, it is necessary to compare its potential with those of the various simpler models used in the past. We must therefore return to the body of clinical data already conceptualized in accord with the topographic, tripartite, and reflex arc models. It should be recalled that the purpose of this demonstration is confined to testing how far each model can go in facilitating the reduction and ordering of clinical observations. In this chapter we will no longer consider the rationale which led us to devise the hierarchical model.

FIRST ILLUSTRATION: THE RAT MAN

In chapter 2 we used Freud's classical case study of the Rat Man (1909d) to illustrate the explanatory potential of the topographic model. We noted that Freud had already indicated in 1909 that this conceptual tool was not entirely adequate for the clarification of some of his observations in this case, and that he ended his account with an impressionistic description of just these features of the patient. Freud's portrait came close to formulating the problem in the terms that the tripartite model was to embody. Freud showed that the usual mode of this patient's psychic organization involved the cluster: repression—moral anxiety—ego ideal—reality principle—Mode IV in our schema.

At this point we shall concentrate on still other aspects of the data in the case history which fall outside of this characteristic cluster. In doing this we must emphasize that the "enlightened and superior" Rat Man always looked upon his obsessions and their magical underpinnings as irrational, as alien intrusions into his mental life. The patient's reality testing was always unimpaired. The principal mode of his personality organization in adult life remained that of a person who has achieved Oedipal resolution. Although more regressive modes also continued to play a role in his mental life, in his overall organization he never regressed from the achievements of this developmental step. In terms of the hierarchical model, the Rat Man always remained within Phase IV.[1] The hierarchical model is the only conceptual tool which is capable of indicating the distinction between the use of regressive modes within a stable phasic organization, as exemplified by the Rat Man, and structural regressions of a more global kind in which overall organization returns to the conditions of an earlier phase.[2]

The outstanding regressive features in the case of the Rat Man were the overt occurrence of magical thinking and of aspects of the grandiose self. It must be concluded that a substantial nucleus of the self had escaped the sway of the synthetic function; another way of putting this is that a chronic split in the psyche persisted into adult life. Splits of this kind correspond to Freud's concept of disavowal; Kohut (1971) has called them "vertical splits." They are to be differentiated from personality splits caused by repression, usually represented in models of the mind through the repression barrier (cf. Basch 1967; Modell 1968, pp. 100–102).

The clinical evidence for these interpretations of the Rat Man's personality has been cited in Zetzel's reconsideration of the case at the 1965 Amsterdam Congress. The utilization of disavowal, in addition to that of repression, was proved by the fact that in one portion of his mind the patient showed "inability genuinely to recognize, grieve, or accept the finality of his father's death." Zetzel quoted from Freud's notes:

I pointed out to him that his attempt to deny the reality of his father's death was the whole basis of his neurosis (p. 300).

Zetzel has also made the plausible conjecture that disavowal had continued in operation because in childhood the Rat Man had been unable to deal with the trauma of his sister's death; presumably this inability had resulted from his experiencing his sexual and hostile impulses as the causative agents of the tragedy. Consequently, one portion of the personality would have failed to participate in his general psychic development. It would then have continued to function at the level of organization of the infantile neurosis (in Mode III of our schema). It was this mode of operation that came to the surface, albeit with isolation of affect, in the course of the neurosis in adult life, as the "evil and passionate" unconscious personality described by Freud.

Because these regressive features of the personality were encapsulated by means of various ego defenses in adult life, they can be conceptualized most economically in the theoretical framework of intrapsychic conflicts, as in Freud's concluding section of the original case presentation. For this specific purpose, then, the utilization of the tripartite model would be optimal. In early childhood, these same issues had been relevant within the interpersonal field in the family setting. Zetzel, as well as the discussant of her Amsterdam paper, Myerson (1966), attempted imaginative reconstructions of these childhood circumstances.

The reconstructions may be summarized by stating that the Rat Man's sister died at a time when the synthetic function had not as yet achieved autonomy from conflict in an irreversible fashion. The child presumably responded to the trauma by disavowal, producing a chronic split in the self as the outcome of this unmanageable stress. Such utilization of regressive moves by the ego as defenses against the castration anxiety generated by fantasied oedipal aggressions and counteraggressions is an excellent example of the state of affairs indicated on the hierarchical model when the double arrows running along the vertical axis run in opposite directions, thereby symbolizing that a given function may be regressively abandoned.

Sandler and Joffe (1965), in their discussion of obsessional neuroses, have also stressed that in these conditions ego structure remains intact; changes in the mode of functioning with the outbreak of the symptoms are but distortions and exaggerations of the ego's normal activities. The characteristic obsessional mechanisms of isolation of affect, reaction formation, undoing, intellectualization, and rationalization, as well as the use of magical thinking, are these exaggerations of the usual cognitive and perceptual processes.

The fact that regression in structuralization had not taken place in the case of the Rat Man can be clearly shown by introducing the specifics of the case history into the hierarchical schema. This has been done in figure 11.

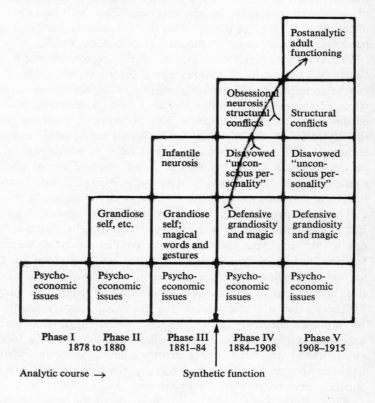

Fig. 11. Life history of the Rat Man studied by means
of the hierarchical model.

SECOND ILLUSTRATION: THE WOLF MAN

The *History of an Infantile Neurosis* (1918 [1914]) contained such a seemingly satisfying set of interpretations of the Wolf Man's character and symptomatology throughout his life that Ruth Mack Brunswick's *Supplement* (1928) must come as a decided shock to the new reader. In retrospect, the first analysis and Freud's account of it must have overlooked certain aspects of mental functioning which had, in the meantime, come to occupy a central place in the Wolf Man's life.

To begin with, the symptom with which the patient had returned to Freud for further analysis in 1919 had been the "hysterical constipation" which Freud had previously interpreted as the repository, in adult life, of his childhood homosexual fixations. It will be recalled that in 1910, at the inception of the analysis, the Wolf Man had been using enemata, administered by a man servant, to evacuate his bowels on a regular basis. On the assumption that the constipation was a conversion symptom, Freud had promised the patient a complete recovery of his intestinal activity through the analysis.[3] Thereupon the bowel became the barometer of the Wolf Man's confidence in Freud and in a short time recovered its normal functions.

The termination of treatment in 1914 came about at Freud's insistence. After this enforced separation, the Wolf Man "had been seized with a longing to tear himself free from [Freud's] influence" (1918 [1914]), p. 122). We would therefore interpret the return of the bowel symptom as a result of the noninterpretive active technique introduced by Freud, leading to an impairment of what had been a silent merger transference (cf. Kohut 1971). In the light of subsequent events, one can only conclude that the improvement brought about through the brief period of resumed analysis in 1919–20 must have been based, once again, on the reestablishment of an archaic, narcissistic bond to Freud, rather than on insight.

In this connection, it may be well to recall the Wolf Man's account (1958) of his initial encounter with Freud: "After the first few hours with Freud, I felt that I had at last found what I had so long been seeking." We are dealing here with phenomena related to the idealization of the parental imago, separation anxiety, and the use of magical gestures and words. In other words, these aspects of the patient's personality were organized in accordance with Mode II.

Freud had by no means overlooked the Wolf Man's narcissistic fixation. He had pointed out that the onset of the neurosis in adolescence had resulted from a narcissistic injury, the shattering of his grandiose illusion of invulnerability by a gonorrheal infection. Moreover, Freud noted that the Wolf Man "looked on himself as a special child of fortune whom no ill could befall" (1918 [1914], p. 99), because he had been born in a caul.

What Freud did not mention in 1914, however, was the other aspect of archaic narcissism, the patient's need for idealized objects. This need could have been behind the remission of his symptomatology in childhood, when it was satisfied by a relationship formed with an admired male tutor. The Wolf Man's recent report (1970) on the beginnings of his analysis reveals that Freud spontaneously met this need through such therapeutic maneuvers as the assumption of the power to decide on the proper timing of the patient's visits to Munich to meet his mistress.

In later years, the special requirements of the grandiose self were covertly satisfied by the Wolf Man's becoming Professor Freud's famous patient. His sense of narcissistic entitlement was further gratified by the yearly collections of money Freud took up on the Wolf Man's behalf, in view of his having become a dispossessed refugee. The same sense of entitlement also found expression in the Wolf Man's concealment of having received some family jewels from Russia, lest Freud discontinue the subsidy.

The second period of relative stability in the patient's clinical condition was brought to an end by the news of Freud's operation for a malignancy in 1923. This event apparently destroyed the illusion of omnipotence required of an idealized parental imago. The Wolf Man's constipation reappeared, as if to signal the collapse of his confidence in Freud. He then developed a series of hypochondriacal preoccupations, mostly about his teeth and his nose. This can be understood as a further narcissistic regression, impairing the cohesiveness of the self experience. This interpretation of incipient fragmentation is supported by the fact that the Wolf Man became severely suspicious of his dentist, as well as of his dermatologist, whom he had provoked into performing various procedures on his nose. His despair and paranoid rage culminated in his return to Freud in October 1926, totally preoccupied with his *idée fixe*, barely aware that his mental state was an abnormal one.

That these drastic developments might have been foreseen can be inferred from Brunswick's later report which described paranoid symptomatology during earlier periods of the Wolf Man's life. These ideas and affects had apparently been successfully encapsulated and disavowed. Brunswick wrote:

Professor Freud has told me that the patient's attitude toward tailors precisely duplicated this later dissatisfaction with and distrust of dentists. So, too, in his first analysis, he went about from tailor to tailor, bribing, begging, raging, making scenes, always finding something wrong, and always staying for a time with the tailor who displeased him (p. 72).

Clearly, Freud had been well aware of this aspect of the patient's character but had not considered it significant enough to include in his report of the case, which had been specifically intended to illuminate the infantile neurosis and its later derivatives. Brunswick, however, was most impressed with the profound change in the Wolf Man's character since Freud's last account. She noted how completely he had come under his wife's control, who managed him in every way. Clearly, there had been a significant structural regression.

These developments have been recently elucidated by Frosch (1967). He quoted and concurred with Harnik's opinion that they represented a repetition, in the transference to Freud, of a childhood psychosis. Harnik had indicated that this may have represented the rageful behavior the little boy had shown during the regime of the harsh governess, at a time when he had been abandoned by his parents. We find this hypothesis persuasive on clinical grounds, but would prefer to state it in somewhat different conceptual terms. The clinical state in childhood may or may not have constituted a "psychosis," depending on one's definition of what this label implies in a young child. In any case, the repetition of the same condition in the Wolf Man's adult life undoubtedly resulted in a psychotic syndrome with great impairment in reality testing.

Once the psychosis supervened, the relationship to Freud and to the various persons who served as substitutes or displacement figures could no longer be properly described as a "transference." Metapsychologically, a transference takes place in the presence of an effective repression barrier; it is a compromise formation which partially circumvents this barrier. As Nunberg has shown (1951), in delusional states such as the Wolf Man's, the patient's relationship to the therapist is a current reality, not a transference from repressed childhood wishes. Freeman (1959, 1962) has repeatedly called attention to this important distinction.

In spite of the regressive loss of reality testing, the Wolf Man's psychosis never involved a return to the conditions of Mode I, to defenselessness, primary narcissism, and so on. On the contrary, a vigorous and raging relatedness to the frustrating object was characteristic of his state, and the idealization of parental imagoes was maintained. We may infer that the development of hypochondriasis did not mean that object libido had been transformed into narcissistic libido. It must have been narcissistic cathexes of various more mature types which had become more primitive once again and reinvested in discrete parts of the bodyself. In order to defend against separation anxiety attendant upon traumatic disillusionment, the patient succeeded in preserving his vital relationship to Freud through the extensive use of projection. He attributed all imperfection and malevolence to insignificant others, such as his dentist. What had been lost as a result of the threat to the continued merger with Freud as omnipotent other was the cohesiveness of the self as a psychic system.[4]

Modell (1968) has cogently argued that the capacity to test reality develops simultaneously with the capacity to tolerate the separateness of the object. In the terms we have utilized, following the work of Kohut, this implies the capacity to tolerate the narcissistic injury of disillusioning imperfections in the parental imagoes. These views are given impressive support by the Wolf Man's clinical course. Prior to his disillusionment with Freud, the patient's persecutory feelings, or, in Kohut's (1972) terms, his "malignant grudge," had been confined to the narrow area of life connected with tailors. The import of this nucleus of psychosis could be easily disavowed. The remainder of the personality had maintained its cohesiveness and was characterized by adequate reality testing. Thus the use of magical rituals during the obsessional illness had been correctly viewed by the patient as an irrational compulsion. With the collapse of this customary organization of the self, incoherence followed. Thereupon, Freud could be simultaneously experienced as an idealized protector and as the object who had lost his omnipotence. The Wolf Man could regard himself as a man of complete probity, and simultaneously conceal his true financial status in order to extract narcissistic supplies from Freud. The personality had fragmented into a series of uncoordinated nuclei without inner communication.

Further elaboration of the clinical data is unnecessary to the major thrust of this discussion. We have attempted to demonstrate that the Wolf Man's relapse, as reported by Brunswick, can be understood without any reference whatsover to either the topographic or the tripartite model. In the foregoing account, we have only utilized the self-object models for the entire explanatory attempt. We have discerned two distinct clinical states during this portion of the patient's course, the prepsychotic one and the psychotic disintegration. These states correspond closely to Modes III and II, respectively, of our hierarchical schema. To put this in another way, the prepsychotic state is adequately conceptualized through the model of whole self and whole objects; understanding of the psychosis requires the utilization of a model of self-nuclei and transitional or part objects. This point of view finds further support through careful study of the successful therapeutic intervention of Brunswick, the report of which has been somewhat neglected in discussions of technique with regressed patients.[5]

The foundation of Brunswick's treatment technique was her consistent focus on the Wolf Man's megalomanic delusion that he was a favorite of Freud's, possessing a relationship of unusual intimacy with him. She

drove home to him his actual position with Freud, the total absence . . . of any social or personal relationship between them (p. 83).

She also confronted him with the fact that the publication of the account of his illness and treatment by Freud was by no means a unique occurrence. She debunked his delusion that Freud was supervising her treatment of his illness. This line of approach forced the patient to confront his rage about having been abandoned by Freud, not only through Freud's having transferred the responsibility for continuing the treatment to Brunswick, but also through the disillusionment created by Freud's illness. The outcome of these interventions was that the Wolf Man acknowledged that he had a realistic need for Brunswick's therapeutic services.[6]

The patient then reexperienced the childhood feeling of needing protection from the very caretakers who were persecuting him. He felt murderous toward both Freud and Brunswick, but this rage disappeared as he began to feel that she was indeed providing him with the protection he needed.[7] He thus became able to acknowledge the passivity which had formerly been defended against through the paranoid developments. Still later in the treatment, his attachment to Brunswick acquired a more libidinal coloring and a heterosexual aim.

Brunswick's lucid presentation brings to our attention data which, once again, can be ordered adequately without resort to either the topographic or the tripartite models; the models of self and objects have been sufficient throughout our discussion. One qualification should be mentioned, however. Brunswick reported a series of dreams from this treatment which required topographic concepts for their interpretation. We assume that this finding implies that during sleep, considerable psychic reintegration was taking place in this patient during his psychosis. Thus, in the dreaming state, the Wolf Man must have been in the same state of organization as any other dreamer in adult life, that is, in Mode II and Phase V. At the same time, in the waking state, he was organized in Mode II and Phase II. Freud has made a similar observation, expressed in somewhat different terms, in describing the "normal" dreams of a paranoid patient (1922).

We have now presented examples of behaviors from various periods of the Wolf Man's life history. We have organized these according to those models of mental functioning which were applicable to the particular phasic organization which characterized each of the examples. All five of the subsidiary models included in the hierarchical schema have been needed to clarify the varied behaviors of the Wolf Man; conversely, only one of the subsidiary models was found to be truly illuminating for each set of these varied behaviors.

If we now turn our attention from these discrete samples of behavior to a consideration of the entire life history of this patient, it becomes apparent that none of the subordinate models can of itself do justice to the complexity of the data. From birth to death, every person will traverse the whole epigenetic sequence on which the hierarchical model is based.[8] Moreover, in the case of the Wolf Man, this entire range of five phases of psychic organization has been necessary for the explanation of various behaviors in adult life. This finding may not be replicated, however, when, using the same conceptual tools, we examine people with other types of personality organization. In fact, this necessity was not present in the case of the Rat Man, whose adult life could be characterized in terms of Phases IV and V exclusively (cf. fig. 11).

The clinical data we have reviewed in the case of the Wolf Man are presented graphically in figure 12. It should be understood that in every portion of the span of time under study, the years 1910 to 1927, there were behaviors which pertained to all of the modes within the schema. For the sake of clarity of presentation, only the most important and characteristic mode utilized at a particular time has been indicated on figure 12.[9]

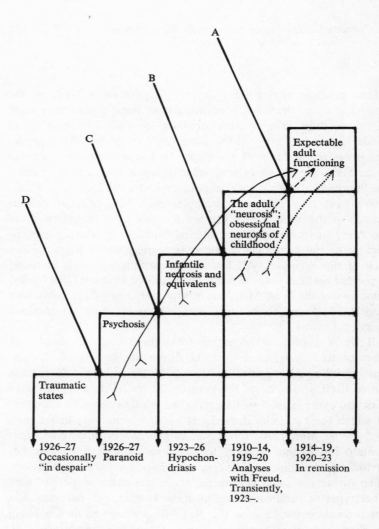

Fig. 12. The Wolf Man studied on the hierarchical schema.

During these years, the Wolf Man achieved expectable adult functioning for two periods: following the termination of his analysis with Freud in 1914, and again following termination in 1920. With these apparent cures, all of the unresolved infantile problems were repressed. This sequence of events is indicated on the diagram by nodal point A, passage from organization in Phase IV to that in Phase V. The patient's behavior was typically that of a "neurosis" (specifically, it consisted of a character disorder similar in structure to the obsessional neurosis of his childhood) during the two periods of analysis with Freud and briefly during the relapse in 1923. His personality was then organized in accordance with our Phase IV, indicated on the diagram by the area between nodal points A and B. This mode of functioning was characterized by severe intrapsychic conflicts; in addition, there were some behaviors which betrayed more regressive modes active beneath the surface.

With regression to a more primitive level of organization in 1923, real dependence on another person became manifest, albeit disavowed. The patient could no longer perform certain psychic functions for himself. Archaic narcissism was overtly concentrated on a phallic substitute, the nose. A similar psychic state had occurred during the infantile neurosis, from the age of four, when the nightmare of the wolves had occurred, to four and a half, when the obsessional neurosis was organized. Both periods can be diagrammed within Phase III, between nodal points B and C. Regression beyond this nodal point C means a loss of the cohesiveness of the self, with tolerance of gross mental contradictions, overt grandiosity, loss of reality testing, and the use of projection as the typical defense. This is Phase II organization, indicated as the area between points C and D on the diagram. A regression of this kind occurred when the Wolf Man was disillusioned with Freud as omnipotent parent; it probably duplicated his condition in childhood upon desertion by his actual parents. If the patient's psychosis had not been adequately treated, it might have led to the repetition of the state of his organization at the time of the childhood nightmare; he would have experienced traumatization through the overwhelming of his capacity to bind excitation. Such a regression beyond nodal point D constitutes a return to Phase I conditions.

We have demonstrated the use of the hierarchical model on a second case example which we have classified as an instance of narcissistic personality disturbance. Others may have preferred to designate the Wolf Man as a borderline personality, or even as a frankly psychotic individual. It remains an historical fact, nonetheless, that each stage of his illness was treated by the psychoanalytic method. It is therefore logical to bracket his case with that of the Rat Man in one functional grouping.

In the next chapter, we will extend the hierarchical concept of case study to clinical materials not usually approached through psychoanalytic treatment. This is an attempt to develop a comprehensive psychoanalytic nosology, which should include the entire gamut of psychopathology, regardless of therapeutic considerations.

9 Applications of the Hierarchical Model

A PSYCHOTIC DISTURBANCE: DANIEL PAUL SCHREBER

The case history of Daniel Paul Schreber is unique among Freud's major clinical studies in that the nature of the diagnosis has never been questioned.[1] While in the extensive analytic literature dealing with the case many issues involving the role of the childhood milieu and the varied phenomena of the psychopathology have been discussed, there is agreement as to the diagnosis of psychosis. While there have been differences of opinion concerning the precise category of schizophrenia or paranoia applicable to Schreber's illness, there has been unanimity about the clinical management of such problems: no possibility of analyzability has been entertained.[2]

It was with this same study that Freud began seriously to apply the tools of psychoanalysis to what had until then been considered the domain of psychiatry. In 1911, he had not yet formulated the concept of narcissism; indeed, according to Selesnick (1966), this theoretical advance was to be achieved only in response to Jung's criticism of the Schreber essay. At any rate, Freud did not yet designate Schreber's illness as a "narcissistic neurosis," as he was to do a few years later. Since Freud's explanation of much of Schreber's psychopathology relies on the concepts then available to him, essentially the transference neurosis and the return of the repressed, certain aspects of the clinical picture could not be fully dealt with.

In spite of this disadvantage and of the fact that the data were not obtained by means of the psychoanalytic method of free association, we have chosen to utilize this material because it is familiar to a wide audience and because it is available in sufficient detail for our purposes, particularly since the publication of the English translation of Schreber's *Memoirs*. Our consideration of the data may be facilitated by a brief preliminary review of psychoanalytic theories of the psychoses, with special emphasis on those of Freud.

In Freud's many attempts to define psychosis, the critical distinguishing criterion remains that of a disordered relation to reality:

a domination of internal psychical reality over the reality of the external world [that opens] the path to a psychosis" (1939 [1934–38], p. 76).

Freud continued to express his explanations of this disorder in topographic terms as late as 1932:

the unconscious repressed [becomes] excessively strong so that it overwhelms the conscious, which is attached to reality (1933 [1932], p. 16).

When he translated this into structural terms, Freud stated that in the psychoses the balance of forces shifts to the disadvantage of the ego, so that alterations or splitting of the ego will ensue (cf. 1940e [1938], pp. 201–2), while the cathexis of certain objects is abandoned (1915e). More recently, Hartmann has emphasized deficiencies in primary autonomous functions in schizophrenia (1953).

As this summary suggests, the crucial analytic statements about psychosis have tended to emphasize deficiencies, absences, or the lack of one or another mental function: repression is faulty, the ego is weak, or neutralizing capacity is missing. Such stress on nondevelopment of aspects of mental functioning which are highlighted in the commonly used models of the mind is of limited usefulness in clarifying the actual mode of mental operations in the psychoses; theory must specify not only what is lacking but also what is to be found.

Freud began such an effort at specification in his conceptualization of the restitutive phenomena of schizophrenia in his paper *On Narcissism* (1914). Parallel concepts for the psychotic depressions were postulated in *Mourning and Melancholia* (1917e [1915]). In both instances, Freud focused on the relations between intrapsychic objects and representations of the self.

Hartmann has also suggested that the cathexis of the self, especially cathexis with raw aggression, may constitute a distinguishing characteristic of schizophrenia (cf. Bak 1971).

We shall examine the clinical data of the Schreber case from varied viewpoints to demonstrate the explanatory potential of each of the traditional models of the mind for this material, as we have done in the previous chapters in the cases of the Rat Man and the Wolf Man. Then we shall apply the hierarchical model to the patient's life history. It will be recalled that the raw data consisted of an autobiographical book written by the patient during a phase of partial remission from his psychosis. In chapter 4, we have already quoted a brief summary of the history prepared by Jones (1955).

Freud's examination of Schreber's autobiography was made principally from the topographic vantage point, as we have indicated. This approach implies taking for granted the preservation of extensive areas of expectable adult functioning even during exacerbations of the illness, and it looks upon the intrusion of pathological mentation into waking consciousness as the phenomenon that requires explanation. In other words, Freud focused on the "return of the repressed," the emergence of previously repressed homosexuality during the psychosis. Freud assumed that Schreber's repressed homosexual love for his childhood father had been tranferred onto Dr. Flechsig at the time of the first hospitalization. With the breakdown of the forces of repression which ushered in the second illness, the love for Flechsig became overt and manifested itself in a variety of ways. Freud enunciated a formula which listed all of these varieties of the possible defensive distortions of the theme, "I, [a man] love him." This formula has become a classic of psychoanalytic psychiatry and the best-remembered part of Freud's discussion.

Freud had discovered as early as 1897 that even "in the most deep-going psychosis the unconscious memory does not break through" (1950 [1892–99], p. 260). This means that the pathological ideas which enter waking thought in the psychosis are in fact distorted expressions of the unconscious. It is precisely the delusions that serve the purpose of providing the necessary defensive distortions in the various forms of paranoia described by Freud in 1911.

Much confusion has resulted from subsequent attempts to decide whether repressed homosexuality plays an etiologic role in the genesis of paranoia. In these controversies it is generally overlooked that Freud made no claim to have clarified this problem. With the conceptual tools of the topographic model, it was in fact impossible to study this issue. Only the nature of the material returning from repression was available for consideration, not the evidence bearing on the causes of the weakening of the repressive forces. Freud stated quite clearly that a different conceptual framework was needed for the understanding of the causes of the outbreak of a psychosis:

a secondary or induced disturbance of the libidinal process may result from abnormal changes in the ego. Indeed, it is probable that processes of this kind constitute the distinctive characteristics of psychosis (1911c, p. 75).

We cite this passage not because the problem of etiology has relevance for our theme, but only to show that Freud was aware that this problem involves issues not considered in the topographic theory.[3]

We believe it is even possible to pinpoint the transition in Schreber's clinical state from one in which the dominant phenomenology was still understandable in terms of topographic concepts to one in which this was no longer true. As we mentioned in chapter 4, the series of traumatic dreams which ushered in the psychosis can better be conceptualized in psychoeconomic terms rather than in topographic ones. Freud noted that the essential outcome of the state of Schreber's psychoeconomic imbalance was the formation of the latter's delusion of "the end of the world."

Freud interpreted such delusions as projections of an internal catastrophe. The "subjective world has come to an end because of the withdrawal of his love from it" (1911c, p. 70). Explanations of this state and of the restitutive phenomena which followed it are most cogent when expressed in terms of the self-object model (see chapt. 5). As a matter of fact, this drastic collapse of the usual organization of the personality, of the self as a psychic system with cohesion, is precisely the kind of clinical event which marks a shift in the regressive direction from a state characterized by a whole self relating to whole objects to one in which a conglomeration of unintegrated nuclei of self are interacting with a series of transitional objects (cf. Kohut 1971; Glover 1968).

There is no better way to illustrate this type of fragmentation than to quote from Schreber's *Memoirs* the relevant description of this process:

the number of points from which contact with my nerves originated increased with time; apart from Professor Flechsig who was the only one whom for a time at least I knew definitely to be among the living, they were mostly departed souls, who began more and more to interest themselves in me (p. 49).

Schreber mentions hundreds of names, and states that these agents caused an unholy turmoil in his mind. Gradually, however, there emerged some order from this chaos. The varied objects of the delusion were classified by Schreber in accord with their benign or malevolent attitudes toward him; Flechsig led the hostile forces, while God himself led his allies.[4] It will be recalled that both Flechsig and God retained the tendency to splinter into multiple representations of widely differing qualities, however. For instance, the "soul-Flechsig" who was persecuting Schreber was not to be confused with the real Professor Flechsig.

Nonetheless, the grouping into good and evil forces was an integrating attempt to bring together the multitude of excitations into a much smaller number of units. Niederland, in a series of papers based on extensive biographical data recently brought to light about Schreber's early life, has convincingly shown the origins of separate delusional or hallucinatory phenomena in discrete childhood interactions with important familial figures.

There is also much evidence to show that some aspects of Schreber's personality, some of the nuclei of his self, continued to operate at relatively more mature levels. One example is provided by his ability to take his meals with the hospital superintendent at the latter's home and to maintain there not merely an acceptable social facade but the behavior of a well-informed and cultured gentleman. Many of his human relationships remained more or less intact, notably his attachment to his wife.[5] Similar observations are, to be sure, routinely to be found in most cases of psychosis. As Freud had noted, an inner observer characterized by rationality seems to watch the passage of the illness from a recess of the psychotic's mind.

In normal development, of course, the sequence would be the reverse of the regressive one demonstrated by this instance of psychosis; we have already reviewed this process in chapter 5. The Schreber case has permitted us to illustrate the change in self organization from a stage of cohesive wholeness to one of fragmentation into component nuclei. It does not lend itself to the demonstration of the progression from fragmentation to cohesiveness, because Schreber, as best we know, was never able to reach a stage of remission from psychosis in which he was without delusions.

In order to demonstrate the relevance of the model of whole self and whole objects to the Schreber data, as opposed to that of the fragmented self and transitional objects which was used to explain the psychosis, we have to examine the period before the outbreak of the major illness. The observations relating to this stage of Schreber's life are scantier than we would prefer; however, they may suffice to illustrate the usefulness of the conceptualization of mental development as a progression from nuclei to cohesion, as first proposed by Glover (1956). The latter pointed out that the eventual strength or weakness of the "ego" (in our terms, this corresponds to the organization of the self as a cohesive system) depends on the degree to which early nuclei retain energy and thus the potential for autonomous action:

According to the strength of its instinctual endowment, to the severity of frustration, the degree of fixation, and the richness of its phantasy products, a nucleus can attempt, as it were, to seize the psychic apparatus and occupy the approaches to perceptual consciousness (pp. 317–18).

Schreber's self-organization had shown its severe instability on the occasion of his hypochondriacal illness, ten years prior to the unequivocal psychotic breakdown. The psychoanalytic explanation of hypochondriasis was not to be presented until Freud's 1914 paper *On Narcissism.* At that time Freud explained this condition in terms of the damming up of narcissistic libido in the body or in some of its organs. Hypochondriasis was therefore looked upon as a *forme fruste* of psychosis in which the cohesiveness of the self is maintained, albeit tenuously. Regression may or may not continue beyond hypochondriasis to actual fragmentation and the subsequent development of a clinically psychotic syndrome. As long as the cohesiveness of the self is preserved, the libidinal cathexis of objects and its concomitant, the capacity to test reality, are also more or less retained. Such a condition of interconnectedness presupposes the state of structuralization described by Glover as multinuclear or multilocular:

Many of the instincts with which the primitive psyche has to deal are component instincts . . . arising from different body zone and organ centers each one of which has an optimum importance, and . . . a specific intensity. . . .These psychic nuclei represent a precipitate of the reactions between the primitive psyche and the objects of its instincts . . . irrespective of whether the actual object is recognized as such (pp. 315–16).

Niederland's investigations have demonstrated the narcissistic fixations which characterized Schreber throughout his life, in particular his need to maintain a grandiose self-concept and that of an idealized parental imago. In Kohut's work (1968, 1971) it has been shown that the need to cling to the idealized, narcissistic object indicates that the processes of internalization have not yet resulted in psychic structure capable of functioning in a completely autonomous manner. This means that an actual person in the interpersonal field has to be utilized as the supplier of the missing self-regulating functions on a continuous basis. In line with these concepts, it is quite natural that Schreber lost his equilibrium on the two occasions which put his self-esteem regulation under maximal strain: first on the occasion of his electoral defeat, and second at the time of his judicial promotion. Both of these events subjected him to increased narcissistic tension through the stimulation and the succeeding frustration of his grandiose exhibitionistic impulses. At the same time, they may have threatened his reliance on an idealized parent because the latter could not ensure political success.

There is another aspect of Schreber's psychic organization which is also best understood through the utilization of the self and object models. This is the characteristic defense of disavowal which must have been in operation in order to safeguard the dominant adaptive aspects of his behavior prior to the psychotic breakdown. Freud was able to demonstrate that after the emergence of the psychosis the typical defense became that of projection. He explained the various delusional permutations of the unconscious homosexual impulse on the basis of the projection of various attributes of the self onto the intrapsychic representations of objects.[6]

It must also be kept in mind that regression to a state of fragmentation of the self is inevitably accompanied by a concurrent regression of the capacity to test reality (cf. Modell 1968). As a result, the differentiation of the self from the object becomes blurred once again, so that these intrapsychic changes can also be conceived of as re-fusions of self and object representations.[7]

To illustrate the appropriate use of the tripartite model for Schreber's case history is quite difficult. As is true for most presentations of case material, it is the pathological that is highlighted in Freud's account; the remainder of the personality, which may have been functioning more adequately, has been relatively neglected (see Katan 1953). Nonetheless, the repeated emphasis on Schreber's high moral character leads us to surmise that examples of ego-superego conflict must have been abundant during the prepsychotic phase. We can only cite an example of such conflict from the psychotic phase, however. This was pro-

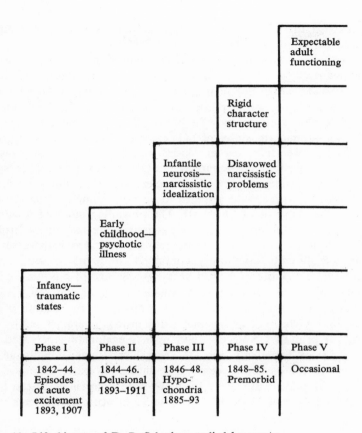

Fig. 13. Life history of D. P. Schreber studied by means
of the hierarchical model.

vided by Niederland (1959b) in his plausible reconstruction of
the dynamics of the psychotic reaction itself. He explained this
collapse in Schreber's personality organization on the basis of the
typical intrapsychic conflict found in persons "wrecked by success" (cf. Freud 1916). This is, of course, a conflict of the ego
with the unconscious superego. Niederland based his reconstruction on Schreber's delusion that his family were margraves of
Tuscany and Tasmania. In this material, Niederland recognized

the wish for an Oedipal triumph as well as the countervailing need for punishment.[8]

Schreber's life history, especially that of his illness, must be summarized graphically in the accompanying figure (13). In childhood, his development apparently proceeded through the expectable progression of phases and culminated in the formation of a rigid character structure in Phase IV. From about the age of six, or around the onset of latency, the severe narcissistic problems left over from earlier phases were repressed or disavowed. Expectable adult functioning was intermittently possible, in spite of the prevailing rigidity of character. The first illness occurred at age forty-three, with a return to an organization of the personality characteristic of Phase III. The prevailing mode of functioning became stabilized around a narcissistic idealization of Professor Flechsig (Mode III), but the more archaic problems revolving around infantile grandiosity continued to be disavowed. These conditions persisted for eight years. At the age of fifty-one, a further regression occurred with fragmentation of the self system, that is, a return to Phase II as the prevailing organization of the psyche. A chaos of unsystematized delusions characterized by the use of primitive projection and open megalomania persisted for the rest of Schreber's life. On several occasions, notably at the onset of the psychotic illness and during an exacerbation at the time the patient lost his wife, there were regressions to the traumatized state of Mode I, with episodes of acute excitement.

10 Further Applications of the Hierarchical Model

A CASE OF DEVELOPMENTAL DISTURBANCE

Ferenczi first wrote of "arrests in development" in 1913, but it was Glover (1943) who conceived of "fixation of the total ego to any one period of development," a statement we take to coincide with the view we shall put forward, although we intend to use a different vocabulary. Nagera (1964) has expressed similar views; he has defined arrest as

fixation to a given phase . . . there seems to be a more extended type of disturbance related to the phase as a whole[1] (p. 223).

Developmental arrests were conceived as a major clinical grouping by Anna Freud (1965). Although any of the individual lines of development may be arrested in isolation from the fate of the others, the diagnosis of developmental disturbance should be reserved for those instances in which the primary pathology consists in the arrest of several crucial developmental lines. A complete, cross-sectional examination of the total personality would probably disclose the arrest of a single developmental line in most people; such a finding is not what we understand by the diagnosis of "arrested development." In our view, this diagnosis should only be made when the crucial lines of development are all arrested within the same phase. As we discussed in chapter 6, the lines we consider to be most important for the estimation of progress or regression in psychic development are those of the typical situations of danger, the typical defenses, the development of object love and of narcissism, and the development of reality testing. The hierarchical conceptualization of mental functioning can be of maximum usefulness in the understanding of clinical problems of this kind. In particular, whenever therapeutic intervention succeeds in counteracting the arrest and in reinstating the progression of development (cf. A. Freud 1965, p. 226), the hierarchical model aids comprehension. No previous model has permitted us to note developmental advances from phase to phase and to differentiate this progression from the maturation of functions which have previously acquired autonomy from conflict. Even without therapy, one sees psychological growth in the areas of function which are free from conflict, so that arrest in development should never be thought of as total.

Because of the relative novelty of its conceptualization as a diagnostic entity, it is rather difficult to find appropriate illustrative case material in the literature on developmental arrest. Moreover, none of the published case histories which are suitable have been given the diagnostic label of "arrest in development." We shall examine one of the recently published clinical studies which fits this category, although it was not seen in this light by its author.[2] Clinical data which were published in order to demonstrate that analytic intervention may be beneficial in certain syndromes of a primitive type, syndromes in which—in our opinion—the nature of the psychopathology was not precisely delineated, are in fact optimal for our purposes. It would be repetitious to illustrate every one of the possible levels of arrest in development. We have chosen our example to demonstrate arrest at a relatively primitive stage in the hope of providing the clearest possible differentiation from other nosological entities. The case we have selected was originally described by Zavitzianos (1967). He presented the initial clinical picture and the past history as follows:

Lillian, an attractive brunette from the Middle West, was 20 years old when she started analysis. She wanted treatment so that she could be re-admitted to college. She had been expelled because the school authorities had suspected her of stealing, and under the pressure of anxiety she had confessed. She had been stealing since age 7, but had never been actually caught at it (or at any of her delinquent actions), except twice by her mother when she was 9 years old. On those occasions she was only slightly reprimanded.

Lillian's stealing was not motivated by want. Her mother spoiled her constantly with money and gifts, in order to keep Lillian dependent on her. It was later discovered that, besides stealing money, Lillian was also stealing women's clothing and underwear, stockings, jewelry and anything else that would improve her appearance. She also derived great pleasure from shopping for such articles and from the spending of money. Occasionally she would steal objects other than clothing, such as books. Sometimes she would forge signatures.

In addition to stealing and shopping, she also lied. She had a promiscuous sexual life from the age of 13; and had, in recent years, been drinking in bars, occasionally to the point of intoxication. Another characteristic feature of Lillian's personality was imitation of the manners, speech and dress of women whom she admired. She especially admired and envied married and pregnant women, and would steal from them or buy clothes similar to theirs. This would make her feel as if she were "almost completely" the admired woman.

Lillian had a strong desire to have children. However, she often mistreated and neglected them, including the ones who were placed in her care. She liked to hurt them physically, to the point of making them cry. She would masturbate little boys and hug little girls so tightly that they would be in agony. For these purposes she would select children who had not yet learned to talk and could not, therefore, complain to their mothers. She also mistreated animals, for example, she used to pull out her cat's claws.

Lillian would also make bold advances to boys, often on their first date. She usually chose boys who were younger than herself. Her desire was to masturbate them manually or perform fellatio on them. During any kind of sexual relation she was completely frigid. She could not become sexually stimulated during intercourse, nor could she develop any feelings. She would rationalize by saying that since it was she who caused the boy's orgasm, his power and his feelings of pleasure were actually hers. She felt that she "absorbed the boy's experience" and made it her own.

Lillian's intellectual abilities were unimpaired. Although actually immature and infantile, she was appropriate in her general behavior and well-poised. She liked to give the impression of being a self-possessed and well-controlled person, free of any emotional disturbances. She tried to be well-mannered and seductive, in order to charm people. She acted submissively, and complied outwardly with the rules of the school authorities, acting out only behind their backs.

The stealing, often planned in advance and carefully executed, was enjoyable to her. She was proud of her delinquent accomplishments and did not experience any shame or guilt feelings over her acting out. With denial and rationalization she easily deceived her deficient, non-integrated and partly delinquent superego. She managed to avoid guilt feelings about her shoplifting and promiscuous behavior by either denying the acts altogether or disowning a part of the self and denying to herself that it was she who had perpetrated or engaged in those acts. A state of slight dissociation, with split of the self-image, sometimes occurred during shoplifting, making her feel as if she were two persons—the nice, rich, high-class girl and the unhappy, deprived girl who steals. The nice girl, whom she thought nobody would ever suspect of stealing, was actually an accomplice because she covered for the thief. Lillian called this dissociation a game.

Lillian was not breast fed. Mothering was very inadequate and inconsistent, and it lacked emotional warmth. There is abundant analytic material and some vague memories which indicate that the patient was subjected, early in life, to masturbation by her mother. She also repeatedly witnessed the primal scene. In her first year of life she suffered a severe pertussis. She was a sleepwalker until puberty, and also sucked her thumb until that age. There was schizophrenia and psychopathy on the maternal side.

Lillian had idealized her mother, who was alcoholic, and who had confessed to stealing in the past and had almost certainly been promiscuous in her youth. She (the mother) had a derogatory attitude toward her husband and was incapable of giving real maternal attention or true emotional warmth. She managed, however—by means of constant gift-giving, false and deceitful attitudes, over-indulgence and over-permissiveness—to keep Lillian dependent on her and alienated from her father. She needed Lillian to satisfy her own symbiotic needs and to gratify, vicariously, her own delinquent propensities. She had a hypocritical attitude—preaching virtue, but tacitly encouraging delinquent behavior.

The father, a bank employee, was an honest man, but weak, self-centered and passively aggressive. He was hostile to the children and often contemptuous toward them. He was little respected by the family because of his lack of authority. Lillian had one period of fairly intimate relationship with him, from about 2 or 3 years of age until latency. At the age of 12 she developed a lasting hatred for him after he strapped her viciously for trivial reasons. She stopped practically all relations with him from them on, except that, when she grew up, she derived a great satisfaction from sharing in the use of the car. Lillian's brother, 3 years her junior, was quite immature, often unrealistic, weak in moral and ethical values. At his birth Lillian became depressed and lost her appetite. She did not complain of any symptoms and her antisocial behavior was very satisfying to her. In fact, despite her consent, she had no intention of actually undergoing analysis. Confident of her intelligence and her ability to manipulate people, she planned to present me with a fictitious case. Her intention was to make a good impression on me so that I would be led to clearing up, within a short time, her problem with the school authorities. At a request from the Dean to Lillian, I wrote a letter to these authorities stating that her behavior was impulsive and that she had started treatment. The letter not only failed to gratify Lillian's hopes in the matter of readmission to school, but, as was revealed later during the analysis, it mortified her because it indicated pathology.

To Lillian, analysis was a humiliating experience which challenged her self-esteem and her magical omnipotence (1967, pp. 440–41).

In a 1971 paper, Zavitzianos added only a few significant details to the history contained in the 1967 paper, as follows.

The stealing, which had begun with taking money and candy from the mother's purse, always involved articles which Lillian liked and found to be useful. Similarly, her lies were either intended to conceal her delinquencies or to enhance her prestige with her audience. Lillian had shown superior talent in learning to read before she started school; she had continued to be an avid reader ever since. Lillian could not remember ever having masturbated. As previously emphasized, the patient's mother had lived out a behavior pattern quite similar to this presenting picture of her daughter.

Zavitzianos concluded in 1971 that:

The general impression at first was that her behavior was merely an uninhibited gratification of antisocial aggressive and libidinal strivings, which would make her simply a typical antisocial character formation. But after analytic investigation began, serious pathology started appearing (1971, p. 299).

In his description of the course of the analysis in 1967, the author had stressed that the patient had been rebelliously untruthful to begin with. Her "oral greed, anal possessiveness, and penis envy were, to a great extent, ego-syntonic." Analytic perseverance eventually led to important changes, however. She began to accept the analyst's evaluation of her behavior as pathological, and she then became afraid of separation from him. Interruptions of her narcissistic illusions of merger with the analyst, whom she experienced in fantasy as perfect, produced depressive reactions. Much of the time, however, she was stabilized, as she experienced the analyst either as her mirror image or as a part of herself.[3]

Her pattern of acting out in response to narcissistic injuries was gradually replaced by daydreaming. "She then started relating to a psychological object which was a part-object, the penis-breast of the analyst (1967, p. 443). At the same time, she began to masturbate. The significance of these developments was more clearly presented in Zavitzianos' 1971 paper. He showed that they represented the reversal of a sequence of crucial childhood events which had occurred in reaction to the birth of her brother at age three. Her depression at that time had resulted not only from the loss of much of her mother's care but also from being abruptly confronted by the change in the mother's body image. This had apparently meant to her that she could not merge with the mother in fantasy because they were in some important respects different. Lillian had regressed at that time to the utilization of books, previously read to her by her mother, as infantile fetishes; she felt self-sufficient in pretending to be reading by herself.

In the next few years, Lillian had attempted to accomplish a fantasied merger with her father, but this also proved to be difficult because of the manifest anatomical differences between her genitals and his. The child had managed to bridge this gap by constructing an almost delusional belief in an illusory phallus for herself. During the analysis, this came to light in the acting out of phallic exhibitionism, as if she had been a male. In childhood, the illusion was buttressed by a stringent avoidance of her genitals which Zavitzianos attributes to castration anxiety. At any rate, it had involved the abandonment of masturbation.

These measures were not sufficient, however, for the preservation of the merger with father; the analysis revealed strong castrating impulses toward him, which were reexperienced in relation to the analyst's penis. In order to defend against the destructiveness of her fantasies, she had to resort to a further regression threatening the fragmentation of the cohesion of her self. Subjectively, this was experienced as a feeling that her body was falling apart. Her various delinquent activities served the function of relieving this anxiety through fantasies of re-fusion with the lost object: "Thus, castration and separation anxiety disappeared and omnipotence and self-esteem were restored" (1971, p. 301).

Progress in the analysis was marked by the replacement of the penis with the analyst's face in the focus of Lillian's fantasies. At the same time, "a more human tone" developed in the relationship between them. Zavitzianos interprets this change as the result of her achieving the capacity to maintain object cathexis in the face of separation. This capacity implies the establishment of a stable internal representation of the whole object.

There followed in the analysis a lengthy period characterized by the patient's increasing efforts to function autonomously. That this phase represented another new development is perhaps best summed up by a dream in which Lillian was walking alone in "a place on which nobody had ever walked before." Zavitzianos noted in Lillian "improvements in the boundaries of the self, in reality testing, sense of identity, and object relations." The patient now began to make finer discriminations about the qualities of various persons, and her libidinal cathexes increasingly shifted toward heterosexuality. After some working through of anxieties connected with incestuous impulses, the analysis was discontinued in accord with reality considerations.

In summary, Zavitzianos presented the analysis of a girl with manifest delinquency who was successfully treated over the course of six years. We shall not attempt to comment here on Zavitzianos' discussions of the technical problems encountered in such an analysis (1967) and of the relationship of the perversions which came to light in its course with the presenting symptoms of psychopathy (1971). Our aim is to concentrate on the significance of the growth promoted in an extremely infantile person by analytic intervention.[4]

This growth can be charted along the lines of development of the hierarchical model from a more primitive phase of organization toward a more differentiated one. As Zavitzianos has pointed out, Lillian had regressed from her optimal level of functioning during the phallic phase of childhood to a more tenuous adaptation:

> On one level the patient related to reality and accepted social standards—though very superficially—while on another level she was delinquent and virtually delusional. The relation to the object was also on two levels. On one level, the object relation was phallic, while on another it was oral and to a part object not clearly differentiated from the self" (1971, p. 303).

Evidently, the regression had not meant a retreat from the phasic organization (see fig. 10) but only frequent resort to more primitive modes available within it. The utilization of these two modes was made possible by a splitting of the self—the defense of disavowal. As one would expect, therefore, Lillian had been arrested in Phase III, which is characteristic for the phallic phase of childhood and in which disavowal is the typical defense. One aspect of her personality was spared the general arrest of further development: because of the special significance of reading and being read to, this and related intellectual functions continued to evolve, and to achieve sufficient autonomy to enable her to function satisfactorily as a student.

Interestingly enough, it was the higher of Lillian's two levels within this overall organization which was disavowed; the presenting mode of her personality was the more archaic one. Zavitzianos correctly interprets the fragmentation of her self, and her use of transitional objects, fetishes, and part objects. The resort to delinquent activities constituted the assertion of omnipotence. At the same time, she was able to preserve the illusion that her parents possessed ideal qualities; this became particularly clear in the transference, when she gained equilibrium by merging with her analyst's fantasied perfection. Her utilization of gross projective and introjective mechanisms for defense may be illustrated by her claim that by giving a boy an orgasm, Lillian actually possessed his power and feelings of pleasure. In this mode of organization (Mode II), her anxieties concerned the threat of separation from the idealized self-object. When this threat actually came to pass, her defenselessness led her to even more archaic discharge phenomena (in Mode I), such as her thievery.

Zavitzianos' description of the treatment suggests to us that the first progressive move was the healing of the split in the self, with a gradual return to the highest mode of functional organization available in Phase III. At this point the delinquent acting out ceased, masturbation was resumed, castration anxiety was experienced, and the analyst began to be perceived as a whole person. Omnipotence persisted in the area of sexuality, in the form of the exhibitionism involving the illusory phallus; in this matter, the defensive disavowal of narcissistically painful realities was continued. With further analytic work, the internalization of ideals seems to have proceeded far enough to permit Lillian to dispense with using the analyst as an external complement for her deficient psychic functions. The best evidence that this step was actually taken is the emergence of guilt in reaction to the aggressive fantasies of her incestuous transference. Simultaneously, her object relations matured in the direction of permitting her to make finer discriminations concerning qualities of the analyst. In parallel with this capacity to be realistic about the object, she acquired the ability to distinguish fantasy from action in the external sphere, and her behavior began to be governed by the reality principle. This change also meant the coalescence of the self as a psychic system with cohesiveness and stability, that is, the achievement of a psychic system able to maintain its functional integrity even in the absence of the object. At this stage of the analysis, repression seems to have taken over the role of the typical defense mechanism. This conclusion is based on Zavitzianos' report that the analysis of incestuous wishes encountered intense resistance and produced much anxiety.

The changes described for the later stages of the analysis indicate maturation of the overall organization of the patient's personality. She passed from Phase III into Phase IV at the least; the termination of analysis may even have constituted some renunciation of wishes, indicating the capacity to function at times in Mode V. Thus Lillian may actually have attained functioning at expectable adult levels (Phase V). The crucial therapeutic experience seems to have been the replacement of archaic grandiosity by the idealization of the analyst, leading to the internalization of more reasonable ideals as the illusions about the perfection of the self and object were gradually given up.

It would not be legitimate to assert that the five lines of development reviewed in the foregoing discussion and included in the hierarchical model cover all the essential issues for the assessment of this particular case history; other lines of development may be even more important to our understanding than the ones we have discussed. However, we have not taken the trouble so to expand this case study because we have made the assumption that most developmental lines would be arrested in Phase III, regressed to Mode II, and so on. The only exceptions would be those mental functions which were not involved in conflict and had therefore reached secondary autonomy, such as the capacity to read.

Our hypothesis, that developmental arrest would involve all lines of development in the same manner, must be tested empirically through extensive clinical investigation. In more general terms, the correlation of various lines of development with psychopathological entities also awaits empirical study. At this time, we must content ourselves with an incomplete treatment of this subject. All we can attempt is a demonstration of the way in which the hierarchical model permits us to differentiate cases of arrested development from other diagnostic entities. This exposition may be followed with the aid of figures 14 and 15.

The diagram of interpretations of the clinical data concerning Zavitzianos' case (fig. 14) is almost identical with the model derived from the theories of psychoanalytic developmental psychology found in chapter 6 (cf. figs. 7, 8, 9). This would seem to indicate that the effects of treatment on this patient paralleled the expectable course of psychological development in childhood. It should be noted that the diagram of the clinical state at the time of the initial examination (fig. 15) is markedly different from those illustrating the clinical pictures of the cases we have discussed in previous chapters, including those of narcissistic personality disturbance (fig. 12) and of psychosis (fig. 13). In these examples (the Wolf Man and Schreber, respectively) there were no arrests in development: each of the developmental lines considered had at one time progressed into its most mature phase. It was only in adult life, under the impact of various stress situations, that regression occurred, with a return to psychic organizations characteristic of earlier phases.

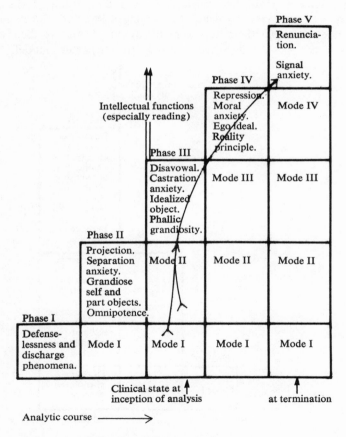

Fig. 14. Case history of Lillian studied through the hierarchical schema.

Zavitzianos' patient had been arrested within Phase III; her prevailing mode of functioning had been Mode II. This presenting picture could be understood optimally by means of the models of self and object. Initially, her behavior fluctuated between relations involving nuclei of the self and part objects (such as infantile fetishes) on the one hand, and self-cohesion by means of merger with an idealized whole object on the other. Subsequent improvement could be measured by the diminution of the frequency of behaviors to which the model of self and object nuclei is relevant, and their replacement by more mature behaviors which are best understood through the tripartite model. The

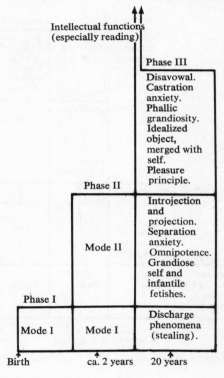

Fig. 15. Case history of Lillian—presenting picture.

utilization of this model before the internalization of the superego would entail the difficulties we have enumerated previously: excessive concern with defects, absences, and lacks.[5]

In summary, the case of Lillian may be distinguished as one of arrested development through the finding that none of the developmental lines we have deemed to be essential for personality assessment had progressed at any time beyond one particular developmental nodal point. On the contrary, there had been some regression away from this highest level of functioning, so that the presenting picture at the time of entering treatment was even more primitive than her functioning at her highest level, except in the area of intellectual functioning. Because of the relatively archaic level at which this patient has been arrested, her case shows a dramatic contrast with other types of psychopathology when compared on the hierarchical schema. Arrests at somewhat less archaic levels would show the contrast to a lesser degree, but the same principle would apply: arrests fail to progress through the usual sequence of developmental phases in childhood. Other types of psychopathology show a regression in adult life to earlier organizational gestalten after an expectable course of childhood development.

Examples of arrests at later developmental phases may be found in Adatto's paper (1958) concerning successful analyes of "late adolescents."[6] He wrote:

From the course of the analysis it became evident that following an intense working through of conflictual material, there was a period of homeostasis and absence of analytic motivation. It is postulated that this represents an ego reintegration which is normal for this period of development, and is a final latency period prior to the attainment of full maturation (p. 177).

Adatto's data may be viewed in terms of cases of arrested development at a relatively late point, perhaps just beyond Phase III, but before final resolution of Oedipal conflicts. Adatto's presentation does not permit a decision as to whether the arrest was clinically evident during latency, or whether it developed in adolescence. Overall adaptation had ranged from barely satisfactory to excellent prior to the difficulties which had produced the therapeutic intervention. It is possible that Adatto's patients did not constitute a homogeneous group in this regard. At any rate, the author stated that: "the transition from oedipal and narcissistically colored objects to mature ones had not taken place prior to beginning analysis" (p. 175).

Adatto is most explicit about the issue of object relations; he suggests that in treatment he had functioned simultaneously as a transference object and as a new real object for these patients. However:

> while the transference is resolved sufficiently to form nonincestuous object relationships, it is still unconsciously only partly resolved. It is not like the freedom observed in the fuller analysis of the adult patient who has no need to break suddenly away (p. 175).

Adatto feels that the newly found love object outside of treatment may catalyze the process of maturation. However, there was no opportunity to confirm this hypothesis with analytic data.

Other pertinent lines of development are touched upon more briefly in this paper. Adatto makes note of "narcissistic identifications" becoming more stable and a change occurring toward more realistic relationships. Defenses are described as having moved from impulsivity to stability. The typical anxiety is interpreted as castration fear. There is little indication of any disturbance of the sense of reality.

Adatto conceptualized the problem as one occurring within the fully differentiated psychic structure comprised of ego, superego, and id: consequently, he is led into the dilemma of suggesting that the analyst is simultaneously a transference figure and a new, real object; that the analyst outlives his usefulness by bridging the gap between parental and mature nonincestuous love objects; and even that a new "ego equilibrium" allows for successful termination after five months of analysis. If the mental structure of these patients did indeed permit internal self-regulation, the varied regressive manifestations observed by Adatto would be primarily libidinal in nature and could be understood to have had defensive aims.

In our view, however, these adolescents are probably more frequently not yet capable of fully internalized self-regulation. Therefore it is more fruitful to think of their functioning in terms of a model of an open system, that is, as having been arrested in their development. Therapeutic intervention had unhitched the arrest by means of the real object relationship provided by the analyst. Treatment had then allowed development to proceed into the subsystem characterized by internal regulation (cf. Gitelson 1948).

The condition of these patients before they entered treatment could be most economically conceptualized by means of the self-object model. As the internal regulation characteristic of a fully differentiated psyche was achieved in therapy, this model would have lost its relevance and the tripartite one would have become more pertinent. If we were to study such patients in terms of the multiple developmental lines of the hierarchical model, we could answer specifically the question of what actually constitutes their "ego reintegration" (cf. Gedo 1966).

SUMMARY FOR THE APPLICATION OF HIERARCHICAL CONCEPTS TO CASES BEYOND THE RANGE OF CLASSICAL ANALYSIS

We have attempted to show that clinical material from cases of psychosis and of developmental arrest at various stages can be comprehended successfully by an approach utilizing the hierarchical model. The understanding of other clinical entities, which we have not discussed, would probably be similarly enhanced by this conceptual tool. The hierarchical model allows a broadening of our perception so that multiple areas of discrete function can be appreciated simultaneously. This is in contrast to other psychoanalytic approaches which focus on discrete areas of the personality, such as the tripartite model which focuses on neurotic conflicts, to the exclusion of numerous other modes of behavior simultaneously available to the individual.

This perception of behavior should broaden our conception of personality, allowing us to devise a parallel psychoanalytic nosology which will more accurately reflect the full range of human potentialities. In contrast, traditional nosologies focus on certain singular features of pathology and lead to a narrowing appreciation of the range of possibilities of human behavior. The nosology and some of its implications derived from this broad approach will be outlined in the ensuing section.

III Conclusions and Implications

A Psychoanalytic Nosology and Its Implications for Treatment

Thus far we have reviewed and expanded psychoanalytic theory in an attempt to bring greater conceptual order to the clinical concepts of psychoanalysis while utilizing the broadest possible metapsychological framework. The choice of significant variables was determined by our stated goal of clarifying what Rapaport (1960) had designated as the "specific theory" of psychoanalysis; that is, the propositions which are based on observational data obtained in the analytic setting by means of the basic rule of free association. In contrast, a "general theory" of psychoanalysis, one that would attempt to integrate these observations with others originating outside of the bounds of the basic rule, would have to include further variables. Models of the mind representing these broader theories have been excluded from consideration in this work.[1]

Clinical theory is designed to deal with psychopathology. It was a regular feature of Freud's methodology to make inferences about the entire range of mental functioning from the study of its disturbances. Therefore, it has been a constant unstated assumption of psychoanalytic expositions of the mind that those functions which are most likely to become disordered are the most relevant ones to study. The developmental lines we have discussed in constructing the hierarchical model were also chosen on the basis of an implicit nosological schema of psychopathology. So that while in previous chapters we have merely attempted to demonstrate the usefulness of this model in studying a limited variety of psychopathology, it is now necessary to make explicit the rationale underlying the distinction among the various types of behaviors.

The four major categories in the tentative nosological schema we are about to outline have been illustrated through clinical examples in the preceding chapters. Neurotic character disorders were exemplified through the case of the Rat Man, narcissistic personality disorders through the Wolf Man, psychotic disorders through the case of Schreber, and developmental disturbances through the case of Lillian. The study of these case materials with the aid of various models has, in each instance, also provided us with opportunities to consider two additional behavioral categories within the nosological classification: expectable adult psychological functioning and traumatic states.

Rangell (1965) has recently reviewed the problems that must be overcome to produce a truly psychoanalytic nosology, one based on regularities which arise from analytic observations and the clinical generalization derived therefrom, rather than one based on phenomenological description. Rangell calls for a unitary frame of reference for the understanding of the total personality. His incisive critique of traditional diagnostic categories is followed by a proposed schema based on the structural theory, listing numerous factors characterizing ego and superego function. We find this proposal to be at the same time too limiting and too complex. It is too limiting in that it groups together at the more primitive end of the developmental scale a variety of conditions creating a general class of disorder in which psychic structure is incomplete. It is too complex in that it provides at the opposite end of the scale a profusion of fine discriminations which become too unwieldy for diagnostic purposes.

Our assumptions for a more balanced ordering of psychopathology are as follows.

1. The position of functional capacities attained along any single developmental line cannot be utilized by itself as an indicator of psychopathology. Meaningful psychopathological constellations consist, rather, of typical combinations of the development of crucial functions.

2. The achievements of each phase of development must be considered along the line of maturation to positions of secondary autonomy from conflict. At the same time, it must be determined how the functions no longer performed by these structures (which have "changed their function") are being carried out.

3. Those functions that do not pass through the gradient from conflict dependence to secondary autonomy, but are free of conflict all along, that is, "primarily autonomous," must be superimposed on a scheme of multiple developmental lines.

These assumptions imply that one must simultaneously define areas of psychopathology as well as make an assessment of the overall personality. As we have shown in previous chapters through our method of case study, discrete areas of pathological functioning can be identified and studied by means of the model appropriate to the mode of organization of the relevant subsystem of the psyche. At the same time, the totality of behavior throughout that individual's life will be clarified through the overall hierarchical schema. For example, a person's wish-fulfilling dreams, parapraxes, isolated neurotic symptoms, and certain creative endeavors may be placed into a consistent framework by using the topographic model. In order to clarify aspects of the same individual's character disorder, we have to resort to the tripartite model. Should such a person suffer a regression under stress or achieve a transference neurosis in the process of psychoanalytic treatment, certain facets of his behavior would best be illuminated by using the model of self and object. If the regression proceeds to the dissolution of the cohesiveness of the self, the model of disparate nuclei of the self and transitional objects has to be invoked. In extreme circumstances, with the occurrence of traumatization, the reflex arc model would be needed to illustrate certain behaviors. It is essential to keep in mind, however, that at any one time the multiplicity of behaviors of the person is most cogently ordered on the basis of more than a single one of these models. As we have demonstrated, even psychotics with a fragmented self who are actively hallucinating may have "successful" dreams showing transference phenomena. In contrast, the hierarchical model can be used to assess the total configuration of simultaneous behavioral possibilities, thus integrating these subsystems into an overall portrayal of the personality. This approach is in agreement with Glover's plea (1968, p. 75) for the establishment of a developmental series of mental disorders. Glover has cautioned that such a series must take into account continuity of mental functioning; such continuity is customarily overlooked in cross-sectional diagnostic approaches. Most traditional nosological schemata disregard the principle of epigenesis in favor of a theory of development characterized by superimposed layers. We find such an approach to be untenable in many ways. We should like to emphasize once again that early functional capacities always persist, both in their original "primitive" forms and in the various progressively more "mature" forms they may attain. Development proceeds by the progressive addition of new structures which operate in parallel with earlier ones and which permit the maturation of the latter, a maturation designated by Hartmann (1939) as "change of function."

Correlation of major psychopathological categories with the five phases of functional organization and the various possible modes of specific functioning within each (cf. fig. 16) yields the following nosological schema, arranged in descending order of relative maturity.

A. Conditions in which development has been uninterrupted
   1. Expectable adult psychological functioning
   2. Neurotic character disorders
   3. Narcissistic personality disorders
   4. Psychotic disintegrations
   5. Traumatic states.
B. Arrests in development
   1. In Phase IV
   2. In Phase III
   3. In Phase II
   4. In Phase I.

The attempt has been to devise a skeletal nosology which is consistent with Freud's overriding stress on the continuum between health and disease. His earlier statements on this subject were couched in libidinal terms (cf. 1905d, pp. 148–49). Later, he put the matter in this way: "neuroses and psychoses are not separated by a hard and fast line, any more than health and neurosis" (1924 [1923]).

The hierarchical model illustrates that any simple correlation of health with maturity and severity of psychopathology with

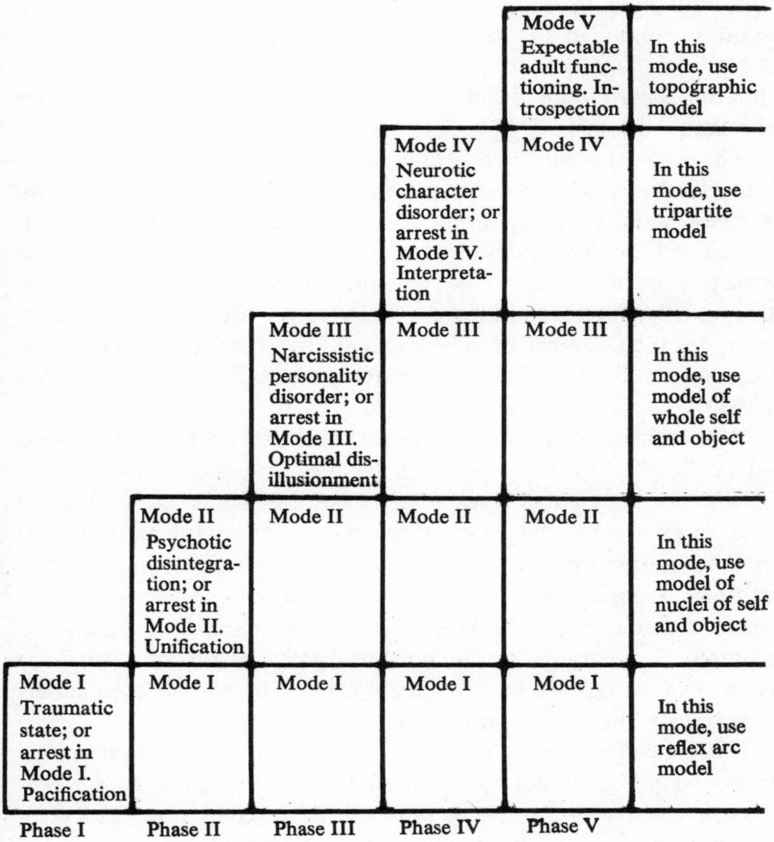

Phase I	Phase II	Phase III	Phase IV	Phase V	
				Mode V — Expectable adult functioning. Introspection	In this mode, use topographic model
			Mode IV — Neurotic character disorder; or arrest in Mode IV. Interpretation	Mode IV	In this mode, use tripartite model
		Mode III — Narcissistic personality disorder; or arrest in Mode III. Optimal disillusionment	Mode III	Mode III	In this mode, use model of whole self and object
	Mode II — Psychotic disintegration; or arrest in Mode II. Unification	Mode II	Mode II	Mode II	In this mode, use model of nuclei of self and object
Mode I — Traumatic state; or arrest in Mode I. Pacification	Mode I	Mode I	Mode I	Mode I	In this mode, use reflex arc model

Fig. 16. The schemata of nosology and of the modalities of treatment, superimposed on the hierarchical model.

lack of maturity is grossly oversimplified. Every individual may traverse the whole gamut of development and still utilize behaviors from each level or mode of functional organization at specific times. We may safely assume that every person has some degree of oral fixation, some separation anxiety, some utilization of projection or disavowal, and so on. Every person may at various times function in accord with any one of the major diagnostic entities, contained in our list of those characterized by uninterrupted development. It is even possible for an individual to function in accord with more than one of these diagnostic entities simultaneously.

The nosology we have proposed takes into account the possibility that in some persons development makes no progress beyond a given nodal point in terms of *any* of the lines of development considered in the model. These are the cases of developmental arrest; with them, only the less mature of the subsystems and the models applicable to these subsystems are germane. Moreover, in such arrests of development, the functions which have been acquired generally fail to reach secondary autonomy (Gedo 1968).

With consistent use of our schema, the assessment of the overall personality would depend on the shifts in the course of time in the developmental level of the various functions studied, as well as on the relative degrees to which various functions persist in their more primitive forms or undergo maturational transformations. Consequently, a wide variety of nonpathological functional types can be described, as well as variable pathological disruptions of a range of functions at various phases of a sequence of developmental levels. This nosological schema has been superimposed on the hierarchical model in figure 16.

Much further work is needed to arrive at a serviceable nosology based on psychoanalytic principles. We have thus far barely outlined a possible method to be pursued in this endeavor. The correlation of the fates of various lines of development in more circumscribed categories included within such a schema and with specific syndromes is an enormous empirical task awaiting clinical investigators. At this time, we shall confine ourselves to a discussion of the implications for a theory of therapy to be derived from the skeletal nosology of mental disorders we have presented.

A HIERARCHY OF TREATMENT MODALITIES

The progressive broadening of the scope of psychoanalysis as a therapy beyond its utilization for the treatment of the psychoneuroses has created controversies about the appropriate limits of its application. Even those analysts who would still confine the use of analytic treatment to the field of the neuroses proper, cannot avoid this question entirely in view of the diagnostic complexities we have just considered. On the other hand, those analysts who advocate the application of analytic treatment to anyone seeking psychological assistance, regardless of the nature of the organization of his personality, can only do so at the risk of obscuring the therapeutic characteristics that distinguish the analytic process from all other therapies. To overcome these extreme attitudes of conservatism and radicalism concerning analyzability, we need an orienting schema of therapeutic modalities appropriate to various clinical problems.

K. R. Eissler (1953) has defined the basic technique of psychoanalysis as one of exclusive reliance on interpretation. He designated any deviation from this model of technique as a "parameter." Parameters have to be introduced whenever the basic technique does not suffice; this is the case when the personality structure is deficient, or, in Eissler's terms, there is a modification of the ego away from the theoretical ideal found in hysterical neuroses. Eissler proposed that the use of a parameter should never exceed the unavoidable minimum and that its effect on the transference must be abolished by later interpretation of the rationale for its introduction. If these conditions cannot be met, the introduction of parameters transforms the treatment technique into something other than psychoanalysis.

Parameters have thus far been described for the most part in behavioral terms alone, by listing various actions on the part of the analyst that have gone beyond interpretation. There has been no attempt to classify the infinite variety of these possible behaviors into a rational ordering of noninterpretive therapeutic modalities. Yet it should be possible to define the main feature of the treatment techniques needed in the major categories of psychopathology. Our guide in this effort should be Eissler's definition of the principal tool of psychoanalytic technique as *interpretation*. This tool should be effective whenever the basic technique of analysis is being applied to the area of its appropriate usefulness, that is, in the treatment of "transference neuroses." These conditions correspond to the category of "neurotic character disorders" in our nosological schema. Every other member of this classification should have its characteristic therapeutic modality. Whenever a patient whose major difficulties belonged within one of these categories was being analyzed, these therapeutic modalities would then constitute the specific parameters needed to supplement the basic technique of psychoanalysis.

Although in practice the analyst usually has to proceed without explicitly planning his therapeutic strategy in advance, he should be prepared to utilize a variety of parameters in every analysis, because the "unmodified ego" for which the basic technique is appropriate is only a theoretical ideal, never to be expected in actuality. With every real patient, problems will arise from those areas of psychic life which antedate structural differentiation; these problems cannot be treated by interpretation alone.

To be sure, claims have often been made about the modification of the functioning of the regressed primitive aspects of the psyche by means of interpretation alone (Boyer and Giovacchini 1967; Rosenfeld 1969). In our view, however, these accounts tend to ignore the effects of such parameters as have been unwittingly introduced into the transaction. We concur with Gitelson's position (1962) that the initial phase of analysis introduces unavoidable parameters prior to the time when systematic interpretations can be brought to bear on the analyst-patient relationship. This is true even in those analyses which permit the utilization of the basic model of technique. Zetzel (1965) has characterized the establishment of a therapeutic alliance during the beginning phase of analysis as a form of object gratification, based on qualities of the analyst which are analogous to the empathic qualities of a mother in response to her child. Gitelson referred to these qualities as the diatrophic function of the analyst. The establishment and maintenance of the therapeutic alliance is especially difficult with patients whose psychic organizations are in a primitive phase or whose major pathology exists in an archaic mode. In our experience, the successful treatment of such patients requires the utilization of extensive parametric techniques.

We disagree with the point of view that interpretation of defenses is the most rational therapeutic approach to the treatment of regressed patients. We feel that it is an epiphenomenon that such verbal interventions are sometimes effective. Explanations based on the influence of intrapsychic conflicts, even when valid in their own right, miss the *essential* processes taking place in these cases (Arlow and Brenner 1964, 1969). In our view, the archaic psyche does operate like a reflex arc; it is principally dealing with the discharge of excitation. Appropriate therapeutic methods for dealing with regressions to this mode of organization (Mode I—see figs. 10, 16), must provide *pacification* through utilizable avenues of discharge or through the control of sources of excitation. This kind of pacification is probably provided by the regularity of therapeutic sessions and by the cathartic possibilities inherent in any "talking cure." If this were so, it would imply that this therapeutic modality may be automatically furnished to some extent by any psychological treatment endeavor, perhaps most of all by psychoanalysis. However, in many instances more radical measures may have to be employed to provide adequate pacification. The use of medication, the provision of protective environments, or even the use of judicious strategies of relative isolation may help to pacify the overstimulated patient (Goldberg and Rubin 1965, 1971). It is hardly sensible to attribute the effectiveness of treatment in a hospital setting to interpretation, at least as far as the treatment of the difficulties of the primitive segment of the psyche is concerned. It is understood, of course, that the same patients who require pacification may also have problems which require therapeutic assistance that stem from more mature portions of the personality. Whenever this is the case, the patient may need a combination of treatment modalities. However, for states of relative psychoeconomic imbalance, the effective therapeutic agent is always the provision of tension reduction and mastery through partial discharge. Such periods of imbalance occur during every analysis. At such times, it is the process of working through that assumes a position of relative primacy, and interpretive interventions are less important.

Profound regressions in psychic organization may stop short of traumatization. In such cases, as well as during recovery from traumata, organization in Mode II may predominate. These psychic states are the psychotic fragmentations of the self which are best understood in terms of the model of disparate nuclei. Effective therapies in these conditions are generally based on the ability of the therapist to serve as a focus around whom the clusters of unintegrated nuclei may coalesce into an integrated, cohesive self. This is not the place to offer the extensive evidence needed to corroborate this hypothesis. As a brief example, it may be sufficient to cite the frequent claim that in successful treatment of acute psychoses reintegration comes about by means of identification with the therapist. From this vantage point, it appears that the major therapeutic necessity for the fragmented psyche is that of *unification*. This can be provided through the continued availability of a reliable object, that is, the presence of a real person or even of a reliable setting. In other words, in this mode of organization it is no longer necessary to provide the need gratifications that lead to pacification: it is sufficient to establish an uninterrupted relationship.[3]

The cardinal importance of a reliable relationship in the treatment of regressed patients is demonstrated by the familiar disruptive effects of separation from the therapist during these efforts. It is therefore somewhat paradoxical that so many purported explanations of the effectiveness of various kinds of treatment with psychotic patients focus on the verbal content of the therapeutic transaction. Yet the seeming effectiveness of so-called interpretive approaches based on widely differing theoretical assumptions ought to suggest that whatever the various therapists are doing right is likely to have little to do with what they tell their patients.[4] It is even more confusing and unreasonable to attempt to explain clinical changes in patients who are lacking in a cohesive self-system and cannot conceive of others in terms of whole objects by invoking the concept of transference and its interpretation. It is sounder to conceptualize these events as consequences of the therapist's entry into the patient's narcissistic world as a transitional object; this intervention serves to bind and integrate the fragmented personality through gradual mastery of narcissistic injuries. This experience is usually not the reliving of any past relationship, however, but a real experience in the present which may have had no precedent. This is why it would be erroneous to think of it as the transference of a repressed past onto the present. It is much more cogent to think in terms of the repair of a "basic fault" through a "new beginning," to use the terminology of Balint (Khan 1969). If the unification of the self is accomplished, there may be additional improvement by way of further maturation of various functions toward secondary autonomy. Moreover, this may lead to the progressive movement of the entire psychic organization into the next Mode (Mode III), characterized by the relationships of the whole self to whole objects.[5] This subject has been comprehensively discussed in Kohut's monograph on narcissistic disorders (1971). A convincing clinical illustration of such maturational progress was published by Kohut previously (1968, p. 99).

Therapeutic efforts in which the principal technical modalities are those of pacification and unification are best classified as nonpsychoanalytic therapies.[6] There are persons, however, in whom the core of the therapeutic task turns out to be pacification and unification but who cannot be influenced without first setting in motion a regressive dissolution of defenses through an analytic process. These are the borderline and psychotic patients described by Winnicott (1954) who have disavowed their infantile "true selves" through living out a pseudomature "false self." Only the exposure of the pain-filled infantile self-experience through lengthy analytic efforts will permit the modification of the true self. As Winnicott has shown, once the infantile helplessness and its psychological concomitants are affectively acknowledged, patients of this kind are often unable to tolerate the frustrations of the basic technique of psychoanalysis. Consequently, parameters may have to be introduced in these later phases of the analysis. Winnicott has called this modification of technique the provision of a "holding environment." In our terms, these patients now have to be provided appropriate pacification and unification. Modell (1968) has echoed Winnicott's view that the treatment must be allowed to be utilized by such patients as a transitional phenomenon (see also Goldberg 1967).

With the progression from relating to transitional objects to interaction with whole objects after the unification of a cohesive self, there is a concurrent restriction of infantile grandiosity. As a result, the personality enters the era of the relinquishment of illusions. This mode of psychic organization (Mode III) requires confrontation with reality as the principal therapeutic tool for the difficulties of disillusionment (cf. Bibring 1954). More specifically, the realities which must be faced are those that have been disavowed through narcissistically motivated illusions. Therefore we prefer to think of the therapeutic aim of confrontations as *optimal disillusion*. This treatment modality is particularly helpful for the problems of adolescence.

The treatment of choice for individuals who aspire to modify their chronic narcissistic personality disturbances, which are derived from fixation in this mode of organization, is, once again, psychoanalysis. A systematic and rational analytic approach to these problems has been made possible by the contributions of Kohut (1966, 1968, 1971, 1972) and others (e.g., Kernberg 1970). Although patients with narcissistic personality disturbance do experience transferred repetitions of past object relations in the course of psychoanalysis, the central arena of the therapeutic struggle in these cases is that of narcissism. The most important issues for these patients are those of the grandiose self and of the idealization of parental imagoes. The grandiose self, although usually disavowed and split off, exerts its covert influence in the form of unattainable ambitions and a consequent shame propensity and ease of mortification. The problem of idealization usually shows itself in the analysis in the form of a need for and illusions about the analyst's perfection. In order to achieve transformations of the archaic narcissism, or its maturation toward secondary autonomy (in our terminology), Kohut has found it necessary to introduce a technical modification into his analytic technique. He advocates the acceptance of the patient's idealization of the analyst without interpretation for a long period. In this sense, the analyst offers himself as a new and real object for the purpose of permitting mastery of a developmental defect. It should be noted that many of these patients are arrested at this stage of development (Phase III); many others have progressed into later phases through disavowal and repression of these central issues in their lives. In either case, disillusionment can only be instituted very gradually through interpretation of the genuine need for idealized parental imagoes. If the technical parameter can be undone through such interpretations, new structure formation will result, and the narcissism will be transformed, leading to the acquisition of humor, wisdom, empathy, and creativity in varying degrees.

Only those persons who have achieved this mastery over their infantile narcissism, either in the course of childhood development or through later therapeutic intervention, are enabled to organize their psychic life in Mode IV. This is the type of psychic organization which can properly be understood through the tripartite model. Thenceforth the ideal technique for the analysis of problems derived from this mode of organization is the basic one of interpretation. This means that ego development has occurred in a manner so favorable as to constitute what Eissler (1953) defined as the "intact ego." This same nodal point in development has to have been passed in order to acquire the capacity to form a therapeutic alliance of the kind conceived by Zetzel.[7]

Mode IV, that of the infantile neurosis and its equivalents in adult life, the neurotic character disorders, is characterized by intersystemic conflict. Hence the principal aim of treatment for these conditions must be the resolution of intrapsychic conflict through *interpretation*. Yorke (1965) has put the effects of interpretation into metapsychological terms: it strengthens the ego, mitigates the severity of the superego, permits small quantities of hitherto dammed-up id energies to be discharged. These conceptualizations show that the construct language of the structural theory here becomes truly meaningful.

For the area of expectable adult functioning (Mode V), we indicate that treatment as such is not specifically needed by noting that *introspection* is sufficient for the understanding of the psychopathology of everyday life, dreaming, and such creative products as jokes, artistic works, and others. Under these conditions, therefore, self-analysis may become possible.[8]

We are now in a position to offer a concise schema of rational treatment possibilities in the full range of diagnostic conditions contained in our nosological proposal. One of us has previously attempted to differentiate those psychotherapies which are intended to deal with age-appropriate developmental crises from those which treat the sequelae of poorly resolved crises from the past (Gedo 1964). Each of the five phases comprising the developmental schema may be thought of as such a crisis. The appropriate psychotherapeutic interventions for each phase or crisis may be listed as follows:

Phase I	pacification
Phase II	unification
Phase III	optimal disillusion
Phase IV	interpretation

In each instance successful intervention should promote reorganization of the personality in the next higher, more complex, and more mature phase. Of course, such progress does not imply that the issues of all previous phases have been perfectly or definitively solved. Growth of this kind may occur in the context of analysis or, more rarely, if the arrest has been caused by environmental failure alone, even in nonanalytic therapy (Gedo 1966).

Most instances of acute regression from a more or less stable premorbid adaptive state may be dealt with through nonanalytic psychotherapy. Such regressions usually involve only a resort to functioning in a more archaic mode, without a retreat of the entire psychic organization to a simpler overall organization, that of a previous phase of development. On the hierarchical model, these functional regressions may be indicated in the vertical dimension, downward, by indicating that the supervening dominant behaviors remain within the phasic organization achieved by the individual at his most advanced stage of development, but descend to one of the more archaic modes possible in that phase. The appropriate modality of the psychotherapy for these conditions would once again depend on the given mode to which the person had regressed: pacification in Mode I, unification in Mode II, optimal disillusion in Mode III, and interpretation in Mode IV. Psychotherapeutic success would then be marked by progress to the next higher *mode*, rather than by reorganization in a higher phase. This is the chief distinction between acute regressive crises and developmental ones in terms of the outcome of successful treatment in each.

As examples of successful therapy in regressive illnesses, we might cite the pacification of an overstimulated psychotic patient as a change from Mode I to Mode II in a person organized in accord with Phase II. A person who usually functions at expectable adult levels (Mode V), but has temporarily fallen back to behaviors best understood in terms of intersystemic conflicts (Mode IV), might be returned to the higher mode by correct interpretations. This may be the mechanism of action of the treatment called "sector analysis" by F. Deutsch (1949) as well as that of the more poorly defined "analytically oriented psychotherapies."

We have devoted a great deal of attention to the theory of the therapeutic action of nonanalytic therapies in order to highlight the conclusion that successful therapeutic intervention in patients with relatively archaic organization of the psyche is indeed possible. We have emphasized that success in such efforts depends primarily on the use of technical modalities of treatment different from that of psychoanalysis proper, that is, on interventions other than interpretation. If the treatment goal is that of attaining the level of function expectable in adults (the characteristics of Mode V), it is necessary first to master the developmental tasks of earlier phases of psychic organization. Because these difficulties are disavowed and/or repressed in most instances in the course of later maturation, these early problems are often amenable to therapeutic influence only through the dissolution of these defenses and the emergence of the archaic aspects of the psyche into awareness. These changes can only be brought about by means of psychóanalytic methods. The analyses of such patients almost always require the utilization of parameters, however. We have defined the necessary parameters for problems of Modes I, II, and III as pacification, unification, and optimal disillusion, respectively. (See also Eissler 1958.)[9]

12 Conclusions and Implications for Psychoanalytic Theory

Although, in a jocular vein, Freud spoke of metapsychology as the "witch" of psychoanalysis, he was insistent about the need for it as a stable theoretical foundation for his empirical findings. Waelder (1962), in his discussion of the essentials of psychoanalysis, defined metapsychology as that level of abstract concepts which lies between inductively constructed clinical theory and the philosophical assumptions upon which the entire science is based. The crucial scientific test of clinical theory is that of truth or validity; for metapsychology, it is that of usefulness and internal consistency. New empirical finds that do not fit into existing metapsychology should lead to its revision. Such changes should be made, however, so as not to disturb the internal consistency of the whole system. The entire set of theories must not be treated as a rigid and fixed system; on the other hand, it is equally sterile for a science to regard its theories in an offhand or amorphous manner.

Another way of stating these views is that metapsychology is a collection of abstract concepts used as a set of guiding principles or reference points for the organization of empirical data. We wish to reemphasize the point we made in chapter 1: current psychoanalytic metapsychology is not a causal-explanatory theory. Some theoreticians may disagree with this opinion and would attribute the position of a hypothetico-deductive theory to the assumptions of metapsychology. We base our views on the fact that psychoanalytic metapsychology, unlike the atomic theory of physics, for example, is still at the level of categorization of data. Whenever concepts of this kind are misused to *explain* processes, the fallacy of circular reasoning has been committed.[1]

Every metapsychological concept must be retested continuously both for its internal consistency with other concepts within the theoretical system and for its specific relevance. In this monograph, we have attempted to submit one series of metapsychological constructs, the models of the mind, to rigorous tests of relevance. Our discussion of these constructs may have shown that none of these models adds anything new to a purely verbal account of the clinical generalizations they portray. Hence these theoretical tools cannot be judged to be "correct" or "incorrect." An explanatory theory, by contrast, would have to be subjected to precisely such tests of truth.

We believe that we have demonstrated that the problem of relevance has been both pressing and difficult in this area of theory. Conclusions derived from a particular set of observations have been formulated as clinical theories, and these have led to metapsychological abstractions. The latter have later been reapplied by certain authors to a different set of observational data without examination of the pertinence of these constructs to this new area. In logic, this fallacy is called generalization—the treatment of separate populations with some shared characteristics as if they were the same population.[2]

There is always a temptation to make abstract concepts and principles more universal than they can or should be. Such misuse renders the concept in question meaningless, often by lifting it to a philosophical plane upon which scientific study is no longer germane. By contrast, the delimitation of discrete phases and modes of mental functioning for which specific models of the mind may be the most relevant conceptual tools has been the major theoretical effort of this study. Our assumption that each existing model of the mind had served well for the ordering of a different set of clinical data but has been inapplicable to others has been tested by the application of the various models to the same case material. We feel that the assumption has been borne out by this test. In our view, the fact that a model has little value in studying phenomena other·than those from the investigation of which that model has been derived does not call for its elimination.

Although we have chosen to study certain models either explicitly proposed by Freud or suggested indirectly by other aspects of his findings, we are aware that still other models have been constructed, or may be advanced in the future. One such model is the earliest one proposed by Freud himself, that found in his *Project* of 1895. We are convinced, however, that these additional models will also prove to have a limited range of relevance as metapsychological constructs. We are thus proposing that all psychoanalytic models of the mind which are valid deserve an equal status. In the same way, the "points of view" of metapsychology, as Rapaport (1960) has shown, represent different perspectives in the study of the same phenomena. We move from one point of view to another in what may be thought of as a "horizontal" manner, without regard to a hierarchy of importance.

Such a conceptual hierarchy does occur in other contexts. It may be exemplified by the fact that models of the mind in general are relatively lower on the scale of abstraction than are the points of view of metapsychology. Gill (1963) has also placed these points of view at the summit of the conceptual system of psychoanalysis. It follows from this that every model of the mind must be subsumed under all of the metapsychological viewpoints. It may be useful to spell out how the hierarchical model meets this requirement.

Because it stresses the acquisition of various psychic structures in the course of epigenesis, the hierarchical model is primarily a structural-genetic one. The economic point of view is considered in it by means of the indication of continuing possibilities of overstimulation. The dynamic and adaptive viewpoints are represented in terms of the emergence of each function from the sphere of conflicts into that of secondary autonomy. The acquisition of primarily autonomous functions may be similarly indicated.

The use of an example may further clarify the distinction between a metapsychological point of view and a model of the mind. Let us choose the concept of topography for this purpose. We have concluded that the topographic model drawn by Freud in 1900 continues to be useful in ordering a certain delimited class of clinical observations. The "topographic theory" as a universal framework for classifying human behavior has been shown to be inadequate (Freud 1923; Arlow and Brenner 1964). Gill (1963), in his attempt to systematize the concepts of topography, concluded that as a point of view of metapsychology topography is not essential. He regards topographic concepts as meaningful at a lower level of the conceptual hierarchy, however. Our advocacy of the topographic model is in harmony with Gill's position: although we have used the model to clarify a limited range of phenomena, we have not found it necessary to utilize topographic concepts elsewhere. Hence, in our work we have not regarded them as one of the metapsychological viewpoints.

Our principal conclusion, then, concerns the need for different theories to deal with different sets of empirical data. As a complement to this, we also propose that no single theory is fully sufficient to order even one set of clinical observations. Schroedinger (1943) has called attention to the error, common to all sciences, of attempting to impose conceptual continuity on nature, which is often discontinuous. His position, applied to psychoanalytic data, calls for the assumption that every human personality presents a variety of behaviors which can be understood most profitably through the utilization of a variety of perspectives or models. Although we have attempted to lay out an overall map of mental functioning along developmental lines in our hierarchical model, we have repeatedly stressed that, on theoretical grounds, this must be conceived in terms of an infinite set of potential variables. It is the necessity to introduce ever new combinations of variables into the model when dealing with novel observational data that keeps our proposal faithful to Schroedinger's viewpoint.

To have shown that each of the existing models of the mind is relevant to a different set of clinical situations has been the easier of the tasks we have set for ourselves in this monograph. It is much more difficult to prove that this discontinuity we have demonstrated reflects a series of significant transitions in the manner of organization of psychic functioning. We have designated this series as the five phases of the developmental sequence, each more complex than the one preceding it. We have tried to show the mutual dependence of several lines of development on each other for their expectable maturational progression. In a significant number of instances, we have shown that progress toward a more mature functional position along one developmental line does depend on the attainment of degrees of maturation in one or more of the others included in our schema. This maturation usually must reach secondary autonomy, so that the expectable stresses of the next developmental phase will not cause it to regress to more archaic levels. The lines of development studied in this monograph undergo their transitions from earlier functional positions to later ones more or less concurrently. We have called these times of concurrent developmental advance "nodal points" in psychic differentiation. It remains to be demonstrated that additional functions also make maturational transitions at these same nodal points.

Our presentation has not proved the significance of the specific nodal points we have designated; this could only be done by showing that the five phases we have described are meaningful for the functional differentiation into subdivisions of every other line of development which might be considered. Such a task is beyond the scope of the current exposition and would require much investigative effort. At this time, we can only claim plausibility for our view that we have demonstrated a series of expectable discontinuities in psychic development. In other words, we see the increasing complexity of mental life with each transition from one phase to the next as a sequence of shifts of a qualitative nature, with the psyche progressively acquiring the capacity to function in an increasing number of modes, arranged in hierarchical fashion.

Of the great variety of conceivable lines of development, we have chosen to discuss the minimal number necessary to provide us with differentiating criteria for a simple but inclusive nosological schema. We have devised this nosology to be maximally significant in a psychoanalytic sense in terms of the differences among its categories. The six sets of behaviors we have chosen for this classification are developmental disturbances, traumatic states, psychotic disorders, narcissistic personality disturbances, neurotic character disorders, and expectable functioning of adulthood. A more refined classification would require the addition of further lines of development for the differentiation of various categories from one another.

As examples of further significant nosological distinctions, we can cite the need to differentiate depressive from paranoid psychoses on the one hand, and obsessional from hysterical character disorders on the other. In order to accomplish this, a minimum requirement would be the inclusion of the line of development of aggression in the schema. Each refinement in nosology will thus produce an overall map of greater complexity. For these purposes, the modes and phases of organization of the hierarchical model may very likely have to be subdivided into smaller units. We should like to stress, however, that such an elaboration of the model would not alter the principles upon which it has been constructed. It is these principles which we look upon as the significant contribution of this monograph: the details we have furnished are not meant to be definitive or unalterable.

The last general implication of this work to which we wish to call attention is the importance of depicting maturation within models, especially to indicate the alternatives of the persistence of primitive aspects of mental functioning or the various vicissitudes they may undergo. We have attempted to satisfy this requirement by employing the concept of "vertical maturation." This encompasses the possibility of certain primitive aspects of the mind persisting into adulthood in an unchanged manner as part of expectable functioning, showing themselves in occasional symptomatic behaviors or in creative activities. It can also categorize the type of maturation which involves changes in the drive component, in the aim, or in the object involved in the behavior, as well as various degrees of dominance or inhibition of the primitive aspects of that line of development. This principle applies to the consideration of a wide variety of functions, ranging from the drives themselves through defenses, danger situations, reality testing, and others. The changes in function achieved through vertical maturation require more sophisticated conceptualizations of health or normality, in line with Hartmann's proposal (1939) to add adaptation to the list of metapsychological points of view.

We shall conclude this presentation by putting forward an implication of the hierarchical approach which has the potential of ordering wide ranges of empirical data. This deductive inference involves the correlation of the regulatory principles of mental functioning with the developmental schema. We shall not review Freud's statements about the regulatory principles of behavior because they have been adequately discussed recently in Schur's excellent monograph (1966).

We have indicated in chapter 6 that behavior which is primarily governed by the reality principle becomes typical when development reaches the level of organization we have designated as Phase IV. In line with what we have stated about other functions, we wish to stress once again that functions typical for more archaic phases persist as potential modes even after the achievement of this more mature position as the "typical" one. Before the dominance of the reality principle becomes established as the typical regulator of behavior, in our Phase III, it is the pleasure principle that is typical.

As early as 1920, Freud demonstrated that the division of mental life in accord with this simple dichotomy of regulatory principles is insufficient for the characterization of all behaviors. To his 1911 definition of the pleasure and reality principles, he added another area of mental life, which he termed "beyond the pleasure principle." He named the organizing force of these archaic behaviors the "repetition compulsion." He attempted to explain these poorly understood phenomena, which often appear to threaten adaptation, or even life itself, on an instinctual basis, by conceptualizing a novel instinct theory of life and death instincts. At the present stage of psychoanalytic evolution, it may be possible to offer categorizations of these behaviors at a level of abstraction closer to clinical relevance.

The modes of functioning Freud had conceptualized in terms of the repetition compulsion reflect the conditions of psychic organization typical for Phases I and II. We accept Schur's well-founded argument that the most primitive behaviors are based on the necessity to avoid unpleasure. It is therefore logical to conceive of the behaviors of Phase I as being regulated by an "unpleasure principle," as Schur has proposed. This principle constitutes the regulator of psychoeconomic balance throughout life and is characteristic for Mode I in all phases.

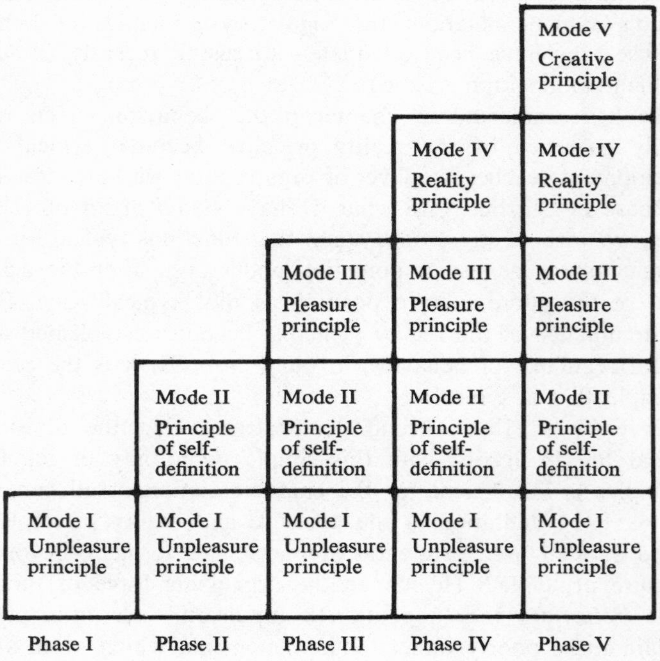

				Mode V Creative principle
			Mode IV Reality principle	Mode IV Reality principle
		Mode III Pleasure principle	Mode III Pleasure principle	Mode III Pleasure principle
	Mode II Principle of self- definition	Mode II Principle of self- definition	Mode II Principle of self- definition	Mode II Principle of self- definition
Mode I Unpleasure principle	Mode I Unpleasure principle	Mode I Unpleasure principle	Mode I Unpleasure principle	Mode I Unpleasure principle
Phase I	Phase II	Phase III	Phase IV	Phase V

Fig. 17. The regulatory principles of mental functioning as a hierarchical system.

In Phase II, on the other hand, the repetition compulsion has to be understood in different terms. The crucial issues typical for Mode II involve the maturational necessity of unifying the disparate nuclei of the self into a cohesive whole. In all phases, whenever these Mode II problems become the overriding considerations, repetitive behaviors will result which have the aim of restoring a sense of self-cohesion, no matter how costly such attempts may prove to be in other terms.

Certain creative endeavors may also fall outside of the mental realm comprised by the regulatory principles outlined by Freud in 1911, but in a manner different from those that lie "beyond the pleasure principle." Eissler (1963), in the context of a study of the psychology of genius, has postulated a potential area "beyond the reality principle." He was implying the development of a more mature position than is involved in adequate adaptation to the existing realities. Eissler believes that such an evolution beyond the reality principle may be the prerequisite for the discovery of novel aspects of actuality. This suggestion seems to be congruent with our schema, corresponding to Phase V conditions within the hierarchy.[3]

Our proposal about the hierarchy of regulatory principles for mental functioning may be recapitulated in brief as shown in figure 17.

In Mode I, behavior is regulated by the unpleasure principle. This is succeeded by the principle of self definition in Mode II, by the pleasure principle in Mode III, the reality principle in Mode IV, and that of creativity in Mode V.

Further elaborations of the conceptualization of psychic functioning as a hierarchical system will be attempted in future studies.

Notes

CHAPTER 1

1. It has been noted (Suslick, in Gedo and Goldberg 1970) that Freud's earliest attempts to describe the functions of the mind in the *Project for a Scientific Psychology* (1950 [1895]) in fact utilized what is currently called a "systems approach."

2. As Langer (1962) has said: "There is a widespread and familiar fallacy known as the 'genetic fallacy' which arises from the historical method in philosophy and criticism: the error of confusing the origin of a thing with its import, of tracing the thing to its most primitive form and then calling it 'merely' this archaic phenomenon" (p. 201).

3. We are departing from the usual psychoanalytic definition of maturation, in which the word designates the constitutionally determined, biological processes of growth (cf. Hartmann and Kris 1945).

4. Such a diagram is not a "model of the mind" but only represents one particular aspect of psychic life. To anticipate the objection that such a picture of a fragment of the mind is not comparable to more elaborate ones, such as the tripartite model, we must ask for the reader's patience, as we plan to present in a later chapter a model of mental functioning based on the principles illustrated by this diagram.

5. For a survey of the pertinent literature, consult Gedo and Pollock (1967) and Schlessinger et al. (1966).

6. Published data always reduce the observed raw material to those of its aspects that seem meaningful in the light of existing theory. Consequently, Freud's earliest case histories do not include enough of what is now considered to be crucial for a psychoanalytic assessment of mental functioning to make them usable for our purposes. On the other hand, if clinical material published many years ago

should turn out to include observational data which are still not adequately handled by the available theoretical tools, this finding should be all the more impressive as a demonstration of the need for new concepts.

CHAPTER 2

1. In German, Freud's word *Instanzen* refers to various levels in the judicial system. The metaphor can be rendered colloquially as "going through channels."

   It has not been generally appreciated that chapter 7 of *The Interpretation of Dreams* also contains a model for the functioning of the immature, unstructured psyche. We shall examine this neglected model in chapter 4.
2. For an earlier statement of these relationships, see letter 52 to Fliess (Freud 1950 [1892–99]). In 1896, the issues were still understood in neurological terms, however.
3. Arlow and Brenner (1964) have tried to fill this gap by utilizing the structural theory of 1923 to explain psychoses psychoanalytically.
4. For a discussion of the "regulatory principles" of mental functioning, with special reference to the distinction between the concepts of "unpleasure principle" and "pleasure principle," see Schur (1966). Freud completed his exposition of the topographic theory by proceeding to define the nature of the systems *Ucs.* and *Pcs.* Processes in the *Ucs.* were called "primary": they are free, timeless, and indestructible; they ceaselessly press for discharge. Processes in the *Pcs.* were called "secondary": they are bound, quiescent, and their discharge is inhibited. In other words, preconscious thought processes are rational and, in terms of psychic energy, operate at low levels of intensity. They may be "drawn into the unconscious" if the energy belonging to an unconscious wish should become "transferred" onto them. This results in the formation of a psychopathological structure characterized by condensations which possess sufficient intensity to force entry into the conscious perceptual systems. The resulting structures have the characteristics of the primary process: loose associations, tolerance of contradictions, displacements of cathexis, and so on. These characteristics are observable in dream work, as well as in the psychoneurotic symptoms formed in the hysterias and obsessional neuroses. In such neuroses, when unconscious contents impinge upon consciousness through transferences, there is invariably some production of anxiety.

5. The patient's death in combat, just a few years after the completion of the analysis, unfortunately precluded the possibility of the study of his subsequent course; on the other hand, we do possess Freud's original clinical records for the case (see Strachey, *Standard Edition*, vol. 10).
6. Further developments in this struggle were described by Freud; see pp. 294–95.
7. Consult Waelder (1962) for a full delineation of an epistemological classification of psychoanalytic propositions.
8. The first psychoanalytic model which took cognizance of an area of uninterrupted access to the depths of the personality was presented by Kohut and Seitz (1963).

CHAPTER 3

1. The history of the term "das Ich" has been discussed by Strachey in his Introduction to *The Ego and the Id*. Although Freud had already given the term the meaning of a set of mental functions in *The Project for a Scientific Psychology* in 1895, he also continued to use it to designate a person's self as a whole. In the period that followed, it was used as a synonym for the forces of repression. The emergence of the concept of narcissism (1914) led to more detailed consideration of these issues. From today's perspective, we may add that the term has been utilized inadvertently for another set of meanings, namely, for the mental representation of the self and for the totality of the psychic organization.
2. Hartmann (1956) has shown that the 1895 *Project* had already contained a workable concept of "ego" in this sense.
3. The most essential references have been brought together in a book edited by Muriel Gardiner (1970).
4. We can infer, however, that he suffered from a masochistic perversion, as he was one of the two male patients upon whose analyses Freud had based his conclusions in "A Child Is Being Beaten" (1919) about this condition.
5. We will utilize this dream in chapter 4 to illustrate still another theoretical approach to psychoanalytic data.

CHAPTER 4

1. To put this idea into the language of the topographic theory, regression in the formal aspects of thinking must not proceed to the registration of percepts but must halt at the mnemic image. This statement shows how inappropriate topographic concepts are for

the description and explanation of the situation in the newborn. Since secondary process thinking has not yet been established at this stage, it is erroneous to talk of "formal regression" from it. At this phase of mental life, the hallucinated image is the norm of thought; it is as yet poorly understood how those more differentiated mental functions which permit simultaneous use of both principles of mental functioning are subsequently acquired (see Freud 1911).

2. Greenacre (1967) has given an excellent summary description of such states: ". . . the severest traumatic situations of all, which are so great as to be overwhelming, tend to be *disorganizing* in their effect on the other activities of the individual. They may result either in states of aimless, frenzied overactivity, sometimes culminating in tantrums of rage or, if the stimulation is acute and focused as well as sudden, it may produce a shock-like, stunned reaction, presenting various degrees of unresponse, inactivity, or torpor" (p. 288).

3. For a synopsis of the case history, see above, chapter 3.

4. For a definition of the concept "actual neurosis," see Freud 1950 [1892], 1895b, and 1895f.

5. At present it is not even understood whether full psychic differentiation is attained at latency, through the identifications which then form the basis of later character, or whether it is only reached with the assumption of adulthood, following the reworking of psychic structure during adolescence. For one view on this score, see Wolf, Gedo and Terman (1972).

CHAPTER 5

1. For a fuller discussion of mental life characterized by the absence of defenses against man's inner core, see chapter 7.

2. A detailed discussion of ego development will be presented in the section on the typical mechanisms of defense in chapter 6.

3. Some of the most cogent theoretical work bearing on these issues has been that of Glover. His views culminated in the conceptualization of a "functional level" as a phase of psychic development (1950). It will be readily apparent that our work owes a heavy intellectual debt to him.

4. Cf. Freud (1909b), especially pp. 41–43.

5. One might say that he had already done so in the *Project* of 1895 in stressing the infant's dependence on adult intervention for the satisfaction of his needs. Cf. chapter 4.

6. For our definition of "self" and its conceptualization as a developmental line, the reader is referred to later pages of this chapter.

7. A further ramification was introduced by Freud (1931a): he distinguished between two types of libidinal objects which may be chosen in adult life. In the first, the love object is chosen on the model of the original caretaking person. Freud called such choices "anaclitic," meaning "leaning on," because he thought that in these cases the libido leans on the self-preservative instinct. In the second type of choice, the object mirrors the self, either in its present form or in a past or hoped-for future aspect. This is "narcissistic object choice."

8. The earliest of these investigators, whose innovative clinical contributions never achieved the acknowledgment they deserve because of inadequate theoretical exposition, was probably Federn (1926–52). The problem was only partially mitigated by the careful introduction to his collected papers written by Weiss. Federn used the word "ego" descriptively for a confusing variety of phenomena—ego feeling, ego boundary, ego cathexis, ego state, and others. At different times, he seems to have had in mind the self (as we have defined it), the system ego in the context of the structural theory, the system *Pcs.* of the topographic theory, and so on. The interpersonal psychology of Sullivan probably attempts to cover the same ground but confines itself to the externally observable behaviors, without formulating a theory of the mind itself. The struggle of the Kleinian school to integrate observations from the treatment of patients with relatively primitive psychic organization into the general body of analytic knowledge has been largely unsuccessful because of the unsound utilization of the constructs of the structural theory for the discussion of the problems of the primitive psyche. For one example of the untenable reifications that may result, see Grinberg (1968).

9. Sandler and Rosenblatt subsume their conceptualization under the structural theory. We would stress that their view is tenable only for conditions following the differentiation of the ego, that is, roughly after the resolution of the Oedipus complex. The representational world is gradually built up at a time when memories are largely organized in accord with their significance in relation to the drives. Consequently, both self and object representations continue to exert their dynamic effects in a manner that cannot be meaningfully classified in terms of the distinction between the ego and the id.

10. For a full description of this developmental line, consult the section on narcissism in chapter 6.

11. This development is discussed in greater detail in the section on reality testing in chapter 6.

12. Kohut's clinical discoveries will be discussed in greater detail in the chapters devoted to illustration of the use of the hierarchical model to organize actual case materials. See especially chapters 8 and 10.

13. For another statement by Rapaport concerning the necessity of a concept of "self" in psychoanalytic theory, see 1967 [1957] (p. 688, n. 2).

14. It should be noted that neurotic character disorders, even when they show many so-called pregenital features in the realm of the libido, do *not* correspond in their mode of organization to that of the phase of archaic self-objects. They remain organized structurally in the mode characteristic of the latency phase. This important issue will be discussed more fully in connection with our clinical illustration of neurotic character disorders in chapter 8. In addition to Kohut's work on narcissistic personality disturbances, important psychoanalytic contributions have been made which have implicitly utilized a self and object frame of reference. Most prominent has been the work of Mahler (1963, 1965, 1966, 1967), using direct observations of the object relations of young children. Jacobson (1964) manages to discuss the same subject matter using the terminology of ego psychology.

15. Goldberg (1971) has applied such a conceptualization of the self to an examination of one significant psychological phenomenon which is not specific to the psychoanalytic situation, that of waiting.

CHAPTER 6

1. Zetzel (1965) has proposed a developmental model organized on the axis of time but otherwise different in its organization from our work.

2. For a detailed discussion of a psychoanalytic nosology, see chapter 11.

3. The necessity of introducing the issue of the development of the sense of reality in order to clarify the line of development of the typical danger situations shows that none of the major issues of psychic life can be left out of account in a well-rounded consideration of any of the others. The line of development of the sense of reality will, in fact, be taken up in detail later in the chapter.

4. Freud had already described the utilization of unpleasure as a signal in the *Project*: "after further repetition, [the release of unpleasure] shrivels up to the intensity of a signal acceptable to the ego" (p. 359). He elaborated this concept in 1900 and 1915.

5. For further elaboration of these issues, see Freud (1926 [1925], pp. 169–72).

6. Note the arrows running in the vertical axis of the diagram. When they run in opposite directions, the particular function they represent may still lose its autonomy, that is, the latter is "reversible." When the twin arrows are parallel, this indicates that secondary autonomy has been attained. The functions treated in this way in this figure are those of the capacity to differentiate self and object cognitively and of the internalization of self-regulation. The unlabeled sets of arrows will be seen to refer to the attainment of a cohesive self and of a consolidated repression barrier.

7. At the same time, Freud made the additional distinction of defining the difference between narcissistic libido and "ego interests": "as regards the differentiation of psychical energies, we are led to the conclusion that to begin with, during the state of narcissism, they exist together . . . not until there is object-cathexis is it possible to discriminate a sexual energy—the libido—from an energy of the ego-instincts" (1914, p. 76).

8. Kohut (personal communication) has called our attention to the connection between the ubiquitous flying fantasies of children and early erection experiences, both of which combine grandiosity with sensual pleasure. The addiction to speeding frequently found in phallic characters may be a derivative of this in adult life. Conversely, fears of falling may represent early traumata which interfered with the child's "flying" grandiosity prematurely, most likely through loss of the support of the idealized omnipotent object. Such fears would then be immediate precursors of castration anxiety.

9. For the history of Freud's evolving theory of female sexuality, see Strachey (*Standard Edition* 19:245–46).

10. Actually, Freud had implied the line of development of the libido in the *Three Essays on the Theory of Sexuality* (1905d), but the substages of this line were not spelled out until later.

11. The question of the achievement of the capacity to distinguish realistically between the self and the outside world has already been discussed in chapter 5 in the context of the development of object relations; it will be alluded to once again in the next section of this chapter, in connection with the sequence of typical defensive operations.

12. See chapter 4 on the issue of the concept "hallucinatory wish fulfillment" as a theoretical fiction. Its use does not imply anything about the actual functions of the brain in infancy.

13. This may be the stage recreated in certain forms of the "mirror transference" brought about in the analyses of narcissistic personality disturbances (cf. Kohut 1968, 1971). The concept is also congruent with Modell's use of Winnicott's term "transitional object" as an intermediate stage in the developmental line of object relations.

14. For the history of Freud's work on reality testing, consult Strachey's Editor's Note to *A Metapsychological Supplement to the Theory of Dreams* (*Standard Edition* 14:219–21). This paper focuses on the problem of hallucination and the capacity to distinguish between fantasy and reality in the waking state. Strachey points out that Freud had already postulated the need for a stable psychic system in the *Project*. This system was named "the ego" in 1895. It was said to be characterized by "secondary psychical processes" capable of creating the delay that permits the perceptual apparatus to provide "indications of reality," thus distinguishing percepts from ideation. Strachey's Note contains a further list of Freud's subsequent discussions of this issue.

15. In 1894, Freud attributed this defensive attitude to "the ego"— a word which then had the meaning of the consciously perceived organization of the self.

16. See also Strachey's comments in *Standard Edition* 20:137–74.

17. For another statement about the varied uses of projection, see Rapaport (1967 [1944] and 1961 [1953]).

18. The fact that differentiation between the ego and the id does not take place until after superego formation constitutes an irrefutable objection to the theoretical option of substituting a "bipartite" model, that is, dichotomizing the psyche into ego and id before superego functioning, whenever the tripartite one is inapplicable.

19. See also Rapaport (1950b and 1961 [1953]).

20. As we shall demonstrate below with clinical material, such regressions may take two forms. The return of the whole psyche to an earlier mode of organization may be termed "structural regression." When selected mechanisms of a relatively more primitive type are brought into play while the overall mode of organization is preserved, it is best to designate this as "functional regression."

21. The question of the subliminal registration of external percepts remains unresolved. If such registration does exist, then only a model such as that of the *Project* can account for it. In other words, separate systems must be postulated for registration and consciousness rather than a unitary one (the *Pcpt.-Cs.* of Freud's later writings on this issue).

22. For a beautiful self-analytic illustration, see Freud (1936).

23. The exposition of these matters in Anna Freud's 1936 monograph is somewhat less clear, for reasons lucidly discussed by Basch (1967).

24. The presence of the phenomena of reaction formation before the formation of the repression barrier is explained more economically through the hypothesis that they are also based on a vertical split in the personality (cf. Kohut 1971) than by the concept of "partial repression."

CHAPTER 7

1. This is not to negate the continued relevance of the psychology of self and of object relations in later stages of development, especially in considering the interaction of the person with his social milieu in the study of interpersonal relations. It is in this area that the concept of identity may be useful.

2. Some of these omissions will be discussed in connection with the problem of a psychoanalytic nosology. At this point we will only mention, as one example, that the developmental line of aggression would have to be included in order to approach comprehensiveness.

3. Modell (1968) seemed to have a similar framework in mind and remained content with the delineation of a schema even more skeletal than the one outlined above (see pp. 121–43).

CHAPTER 8

1. The distinction between regressive aspects of neurotic character disorders and the "structural regression" seen in syndromes of greater primitiveness has been made by previous authors, for example, Modell (1968).

2. Regressions in phasic organization are indicated along the horizontal axis of our diagrams; regressions in mode of functioning are shown along the vertical axis.

3. In terms of the modalities of treatment to be outlined in chapter 11, this parameter would be classified as the provision of a unifying relatedness to an omnipotent and therefore idealized object. Because this intervention was never resolved through interpretation, the technique of the treatment cannot be viewed as psychoanalytic from today's vantage point.

4. For an extensive discussion of such vicissitudes in the treatment of narcissistic personality disorders, see Kohut (1971). We shall deal with the issue in some detail in the next chapter, in discussing

the Schreber case, in which it occupies a place of central importance.

5. For a somewhat different view concerning these matters by one author who did study Brunswick's paper, see Serota (in McLaughlin 1959).

6. Winnicott (1954) has insisted on the necessity that analysis provide the psychotic patient with a setting in which he can give up his "false self" and acknowledge the "true self" in need of early dependence. On the other hand, Kohut (1971) makes a definite distinction between narcissistic problems which are analyzable and those which require therapeutic interventions of other types.

7. In our experience, failure to provide an adequate setting for the patient in such critical contingencies produces a traumatic state, a further regression to Mode I, characterized by defenselessness, overstimulation, and primary narcissism.

8. This statement needs qualification: there are in fact people who fail to make this expectable progression in development; instances of such arrest in development will be discussed in the next chapter. In a future psychoanalytic nosology, persons who fail to complete the phasic progression in development and those who require the full gamut of hierarchical phases for the understanding of their adult behaviors should probably be placed in special categories of psychopathology.

9. It should be kept in mind that diagrams such as figures 11 and 12 are not "models" of psychic function. They are organized on the same basis as the hierarchical model, and each of their boxes is to be understood as corresponding to a particular stage along the lines of development comprising the model, that is, to the stage which occupies the analogous position in the model. However, these diagrams are but summaries of clinical interpretations about a single person and therefore cannot be generalized into a theory. On the basis of data organized in a comparable manner from a wide variety of cases scrutinized in analysis, inductive generalizations could be made from which clinical theories might be constructed.

CHAPTER 9

1. As stated in connection with the previous case examples, the reader may follow our exposition better after refreshing his recollection of the case history by consulting the original sources. See also our summary of the Schreber case in chapter 4.

2. Of this extensive literature, we can cite only a sampling: Baumeyer (1956), Katan (1949, 1950, 1953, 1959), Kohut (1960), Niederland (1951, 1959a, 1959b, 1960, 1963), and White (1961, 1963).

3. It should also be noted that the meaning of the term "ego" in this citation from 1911 is by no means self-evident. It is quite possible that it was being utilized by Freud in the sense of a coherent set of personality functions, in accord with its later usage in the structural theory. On the other hand, it may simply have been used here as a synonym for the self.

4. We assume that this is an example of the mental operations subsumed under the term "splitting" in the writings of Melanie Klein and her school. For a discussion of Kleinian views on object relations, consult chapter 5.

5. This is an impressive demonstration of the fact that there is no inconsistency in making a diagnosis of psychosis in the presence of adequate capacity for object love. The regression which eventuates in the appearance of overt signs of archaic narcissism is not from the libidinal cathexis of objects but from more mature forms of narcissism. It is essential to distinguish object love from object relationships in order to be able to determine whether a particular interaction between a person and others in his interpersonal milieu lies primarily in the realm of narcissism or in that of object libido. For details, see Kohut 1971.

6. Freud was careful to indicate, however, that projection is an ubiquitous defense, found even in normal persons. As Jacobson (1964) has pointed out, projection has its precursors in early infantile incorporation and ejection fantasies. When structuralization has reached the stage of the complete differentiation of the ego, that is, once the tripartite model has become the most relevant one, projection takes its place in the defensive repertory of the ego. As we have stressed, mental mechanisms continue their particular line of development beyond the area of conflicts; when projection reaches the stage of conflict-free organization, it comes to underlie such functions as that of empathy.

7. In *Some Neurotic Mechanisms in Jealousy, Paranoia and Homosexuality* (1922), Freud described a young man whose paranoid psychopathology became apparent only in the course of his analysis: "His actual relations with men were clearly dominated by suspiciousness; his keen intellect easily rationalized this attitude, and he knew how to bring it about that both friends and acquaintances deceived and exploited him. The new thing I learned from studying him was that classical persecutory ideas may be present without finding belief or acceptance . . . it may be that the delusions which we regard as new formations when the disease breaks out have already been long in existence" (p. 228).

In this passage, Freud came very close to the explicit formulation of the concept of a nucleus of the self that may remain submerged or isolated as long as a total synthesis remains in effect. He went on to discuss the "economic issue"—what we might now think of as the question of the relative adaptive capacity of the personality to deal with a motivational impetus which the ego correctly identifies as pathological. These are problems best handled conceptually through utilization of the adaptive point of view and a psychology of the self.

8. The delusion about margraves of Tuscany indicates an Oedipal victory because of Schreber's political opposition to the master of Germany, Bismarck. It was the marchioness Mathilde of Tuscany who had humiliated an emperor of Germany at Canossa in one of the most celebrated episodes of medieval history. Similarly, the reference to Tasmania has the significance of guilt and expiation because this province had originally been utilized as a penal colony.

CHAPTER 10

1. Others who seem to hold similar convictions but have not been quite as explicit in stating them are Winnicott (1965) and M. Khan (1966). See also Nagera (1966); Gedo (1966, 1967, 1968) has made previous efforts to clarify the concept in the context of considering treatment possibilities.

2. Equally suitable reports are those of Ludowyk–Gyomroi (1963) and Tolpin (1971). See Gedo (1967) for a discussion of Ludowyk–Gyomroi's patient as an instance of developmental arrest.

3. Kohut (1968, 1971) has described in detail the propensity of patients with narcissistic personality disturbances to form transferences in which the analyst, as idealized and omnipotent parental imago, is used—generally in a covert, silent manner—for the purpose of fusion (the "merger transference") or for the confirmation of the patient's perfection by mirroring identical qualities (the "twinship transference").

4. Whatever questions the reader may have about the patient's diagnosis or treatment are not of primary relevance at *this* point, as our purpose here is to demonstrate the utility of studying analytic data with the use of the hierarchical concept.

5. The admonition of Hartmann and Loewenstein (1962) that our theory must never neglect the distinction between current function and its genesis can be recalled with profit here.

6. The case presentations are too condensed to allow for a detailed examination of the individual pathology. As a group however, these analyses were of relatively short duration (ten months, five months, several months); the analyst had used some parameters

("intervening on his behalf with his mother"); termination usually occurred with the formation of some new, extra-analytic relationship ("turned toward his girlfriend," "proceeded with her marriage," "committed to his girlfriend").

CHAPTER 11

1. It is instructive to compare models of mental functioning culled from Freud's clinical work, as we have done in this monograph, with the set of models selected by Rapaport (1960, pp. 20–24) in his attempt to systematize the general theory of psychoanalysis. For other attempts to develop a model of universal scope, see Gill (1963) and Arlow and Brenner (1964). In this work we have not taken any position concerning the still controversial issue of whether psychoanalytic theory can or should attempt to form a general theory of psychology. It remains an open question whether such an effort would necessitate interdigitation with the social and biological fields or whether a meaningful solution of this dilemma could be reached through a systems approach such as we have utilized for the more limited purpose of ordering psychoanalytic theory within its own boundaries.

2. This category forms an exception to the ordering of the nosological schema in terms of relative maturity and has therefore been separated as a parallel series. It is quite difficult at times to distinguish between arrests in development and other pathological entities which show many features that derive from the same archaic mode in which the arrest has occurred. For the distinction between arrest and regression, see Modell (1968, p. 126n.). See also our discussion of the issue in chapter 10.

3. The copious literature of group therapy, which we cannot review here, and its claims of therapeutic effectiveness with psychotic patients may gain a new dimension of understanding from the principle of unification and that of tension discharge.

4. Among the divergent schools of psychoanalysis, the most significant for their work in this area are those of Sullivan and of Melanie Klein. Both groups have developed reductionistic theories based on their experiences in treating patients with primitive psychic organization. Both groups have been unable meaningfully to correlate these findings with data from the analysis of transference neuroses because of the lack of a developmental model which could show the hierarchical interrelatedness of these two sets of observations. Instead of such needed correlations, these schools have incorrectly presented these disparate phenomena in terms of identical explanations. Their accounts can be appreciated more properly as descriptions of successful treatment rather than as theoretical contributions.

5. As we have noted in chapter 5, the self and the object are not yet functionally separate at this stage, although each has become unified into a single entity. This state can be represented by the typographical arrangement "self-object" (cf. Kohut 1971).
6. For a fuller classification of psychological therapies, see Gedo (1964).
7. Zetzel's definition (1965) of indications for analysis seems quite narrow until one reminds oneself that she was discussing the use of the basic technique. We would prefer to include well-defined parametric technique within the bounds of psychoanalysis proper, necessitating a broader view of the indications for analysis at the same time.
8. The judgment that treatment is not needed does not imply that the person would not benefit from psychoanalysis, which has the capacity to correct latent problems in every mode of the psychic hierarchy. Similarly, the scientific conclusions of applied psychoanalysis about man's creative products need confirmation from the study of their creators by means of the psychoanalytic method itself.
9. The foregoing discussion deliberately omits consideration of the many treatments in which the therapist correctly avoids dealing with the core issues of the psychopathology. For some of these problems, see Gedo (1964).

CHAPTER 12

1. For a tentative supraordinate explanatory theory of mental function, see Langer (1967).
2. One common and gross instance of this error is the application of metapsychological propositions about intrapsychic phenomena to social psychology or vice versa. For example, the general confusion over the meaning of the term "identity" is probably the result of extrapolating generalizations into an area where they do not apply (cf. our discussion of the work of Erikson in chapter 7). A thorough treatment of this issue would take us too far afield here. It should be noted, however, that Freud was always careful to separate these two realms as distinct areas for study, even when he used the conclusions of individual psychology to delve into group psychology.
3. It should be noted that the psychology of Mode V was described by Freud in 1900 primarily on the basis of introspective data concerning his own dreams. These creative products can be assumed to have met the conditions Eissler has in mind in describing an area beyond the reality principle.

Bibliography

Adatto, C. 1958. Ego Reintegration Observed in Analysis in Late Adolescents. *Int. J. Psycho-Anal.* 39:172–77.

Arlow, J., and Brenner, C. 1964. *Psychoanalytic Concepts of the Structural Theory.* New York: International Universities Press.

———. 1969. The Psychopathology of the Psychoses: A Proposed Revision. *Int. J. Psycho-Anal.* 50:5–14.

Bak, R. 1971. Object-relationships in Schizophrenia and Perversion. *Int. J. Psycho-Anal.* 52:235–42.

Basch, M. 1967. On Disavowal. Unpublished manuscript.

———. 1968. Perception, Subliminal Stimulation, and the "Project." Presented to the Chicago Psychoanalytic Society, November 1968.

Baumeyer, F. 1956. The Schreber Case. *Int. J. Psycho-Anal.* 37:61–74.

Bibring, E. 1954. Psychoanalysis and Dynamic Psychotherapy: Similarities and Differences. *J. Amer. Psychoanal. Assoc.* 2:745–70.

Bonaparte, M., Freud, A., and Kris, E., eds. 1954. *The Origins of Psychoanalysis.* New York: Basic Books.

Boyer, L., and Giovacchini, P. 1967. *Psychoanalytic Treatment of Characterological and Schizophrenic Disorders.* New York: Science House.

Breuer, J., and Freud, S. 1895. *Studies in Hysteria.* In Strachey, vol. 2.

Brunswick, R. 1928–45. A Supplement to Freud's "History of an Infantile Neurosis." In R. Fliess, ed., *A Psychoanalytic Reader.* Second Printing. New York: International Universities Press, 1962. Also in Gardiner, M. 1970.

Deutsch, F. 1949. *Applied Psychoanalysis.* New York: Grune & Stratton.

Eissler, K. 1953. The Effect of the Structure of the Ego on Psychoanalytic Technique. *J. Amer. Psychoanal. Assoc.* 1:104–43.

————. 1958. Notes of Problems of Technique in the Psychoanalytic Treatment of Adolescents: With Some Remarks on Perversions. *Psychoanal. Study of the Child* 13:223–54.

————. 1963. Tentative Notes on the Psychology of Genius. In *Goethe: a Psychoanalytic Study*. Detroit: Wayne State University Press.

Erikson, E. 1958. *Young Man Luther: A Study in Psychoanalysis and History*. New York: W. W. Norton.

————. 1959. *Identity and the Life Cycle*. Psychological Issues, Monograph 1. New York: International Universities Press.

Fairbairn, W. 1954. *An Object Relation Theory of Personality*. New York: Basic Books.

Federn, P. 1926–52. *Ego Psychology and the Psychoses*. Ed. E. Weiss. New York: Basic Books, 1952.

Ferenczi, S. 1911. On Obscene Words. In *Selected Papers of Sandor Ferenczi*, 3 volumes. New York: Basic Books, 1950–55. Vol. 1:132–53.

————. 1913. Stages in the Development of the Sense of Reality. In *Selected Papers*, vol. 1:213–39.

————. 1926. Review of O. Rank: "Technique of Psychoanalysis." *Int. J. Psycho-Anal.* 8:93–100.

Frank, A., and Muslin, H. 1967. The Development of Freud's Concept of Primal Repression. *Psychoanalytic Study of the Child* 22:55–76.

Freeman, T. 1959. Aspects of Defense in Neurosis and Psychosis. *Int. J. Psycho-Anal.* 40:199–212.

————. 1962. Narcissism and Defensive Processes in Schizophrenic States. *Int. J. Psycho-Anal.* 43:415–25.

Freud, A. 1936. *The Ego and the Mechanisms of Defence*. New York: International Universities Press, 1946.

————. 1965. *Normality and Pathology in Childhood*. New York: International Universities Press.

Freud, S. 1940–41 (1892). Sketches for the "Preliminary Communication" of 1893. *Standard Edition* 1:147–54.

————. 1950 (1892–99). Extracts from the Fliess Papers. *Standard Edition* 1:177–280.

————. 1894. The Neuropsychoses of Defence. *Standard Edition* 3:45–61.

————. 1950 (1895). Project for a Scientific Psychology. *Standard Edition* 1:295–391.

————. 1896. Further Remarks on the Neuropsychoses of Defence. *Standard Edition* 3:162–85.

————. 1899. Screen Memories. *Standard Edition* 3:303–22.

————. 1900. The Interpretation of Dreams. *Standard Edition* 4 and 5.

————. 1901. The Psychopathology of Everyday Life. *Standard Edition* 6.

————. 1905c. Jokes and Their Relation to the Unconscious. *Standard Edition* 8.

————. 1905d. Three Essays on the Theory of Sexuality. *Standard Edition* 7:130–243.

————. 1909b. Analysis of a Phobia in a Five-Year-Old Boy. *Standard Edition* 10:5–149.

————. 1909d. Notes Upon a Case of Obsessional Neurosis. *Standard Edition* 10:155–249.

————.1911b. Formulations on the Two Principles of Mental Functioning. *Standard Edition* 12:218–26.

————. 1911c. Psycho-Analytic Notes on an Autobiographical Account of a Case of Paranoia (Dementia Paranoides). *Standard Edition* 12:9–82.

————. 1913 (1912–13). Totem and Taboo. *Standard Edition* 13:1–161.

————. 1914. On Narcissism: An Introduction. *Standard Edition* 14:73–102.

————. 1918 (1914). From the History of an Infantile Neurosis. *Standard Edition* 17:3–122.

————. 1915d. Repression. *Standard Edition* 14:146–58.

————. 1915e. The Unconscious. *Standard Edition* 14:166–204.

————. 1917d (1915). A Metapsychological Supplement to the Theory of Dreams. *Standard Edition* 14:222–35.

————. 1917e (1915). Mourning and Melancholia. *Standard Edition* 14:243–58.

————. 1916. Some Character Types Met with in Psycho-Analytic Work. *Standard Edition* 14:311–33.

————. 1919. "A Child Is Being Beaten." A contribution to the Study of the Origin of Sexual Perversions. *Standard Edition* 17:179–204.

————. 1920. Beyond the Pleasure Principle. *Standard Edition* 18:7–64.

————. 1921. Group Psychology and the Analysis of the Ego. *Standard Edition* 18:69–143.

————. 1922. Some Neurotic Mechanisms in Jealousy, Paranoia, and Homosexuality. *Standard Edition* 18:223–32.

————. 1923b. The Ego and the Id. *Standard Edition* 19:12–59.

————. 1923e. The Infantile Genital Organizations: An Interpolation into the Theory of Sexuality. *Standard Edition* 19:141–48.

———. 1924 (1923). A Short Account of Psycho-Analysis. *Standard Edition* 19:191–209.

———. 1924c. The Economic Problem of Masochism. *Standard Edition* 19:159–70.

———. 1924d. The Dissolution of the Oedipus Complex. *Standard Edition* 19:173–79.

———. 1925. Some Psychical Consequences of the Anatomical Distinction Between the Sexes. *Standard Edition* 19:248–58.

———. 1926 (1925). Inhibitions, Symptoms and Anxiety. *Standard Edition* 20:87–172.

———. 1927. Fetishism. *Standard Edition* 21:152–57.

———. 1931a. Libidinal Types. *Standard Edition* 21:215–20.

———. 1931b. Female Sexuality. *Standard Edition* 21:225–43.

———. 1933 (1932). New Introductory Lectures on Psycho-Analysis. *Standard Edition* 22:5–182.

———. 1939 (1934–38). Moses and Monotheism. *Standard Edition* 23:7–137.

———. 1936. A Disturbance of Memory on the Acropolis. *Standard Edition* 22:239–48.

———. 1937. Analysis Terminable and Interminable. *Standard Edition* 23:216–53.

———. 1940a (1938). An Outline of Psycho-Analysis. *Standard Edition* 23:144–207.

Frosch, J. 1967. Severe Regressive States During Analysis: Introduction. *J. Amer. Psychoanal. Assoc.* 15:491–507.

Gardiner, M. 1952. Meetings with the Wolf Man. *Bulletin Menninger Clinic* 2:17–41. Also in Gardiner, M. 1970.

———. 1964. The Wolf Man Grows Older. *J. Amer. Psychoanal. Assn.* 12:80–92. Also in Gardiner, M. 1970.

Gardiner, M. 1970. *The Wolf Man.* New York: Basic Books.

Gardiner, M., and Augenfeld, M. 1961. Memoirs 1914–1919. *Bulletin Phila. Assoc. Psychoanal.* 11:1–31. Also in Gardiner, M. 1970.

———. 1964. Memoirs 1905–1908. *Bulletin Phila. Assoc. Psychoanal.* 14:80–103. Also in Gardiner, M. 1970.

Gedo, J. 1964. Concepts for a Classification of the Psychotherapies. *Int. J. Psycho-Anal.* 45:530–39.

———. 1966. The Psychotherapy of Developmental Arrest. *Brit. J. Med. Psych.* 39:25–33.

———. 1967. On Critical Periods for Corrective Experience in the Therapy of Arrested Development. *Brit. J. Med. Psych.* 40:79–83.

———. 1968. Toward a Developmental Psychopathology. Abstract by S. Siegel. *Bulletin Phila. Assoc. Psychoanal.* 18:48–52.

———. 1971. A Hierarchical Model of the Modes of Mental Functioning Observed in Psychoanalysis. In Abrams, S. (Reporter). Panel on "Models of the Psychic Apparatus." *J. Amer. Psychoanal. Assoc.* 19:131–42.

Gedo, J., and Goldberg, A. 1970. Models of the Mind in Psychoanalysis. Abstract by J. Handler. *Bulletin Phila. Assoc. Psychoanal.* 20:74–79.

Gedo, J., and Pollock, G. 1967. The Question of Research in Psychoanalytic Technique. In B. Wolman, ed. *Psychoanalytic Techniques.* New York: Basic Books, pp. 560–81.

Gedo, J., Sabshin, M., Sadow, L., and Schlessinger, N. 1964. "Studies in Hysteria": A Methodological Evaluation. *J. Amer. Psychoanal. Assoc.* 12:734–51.

Gill, M. 1963. *Topography and Systems in Psychoanalytic Theory.* Psychological Issues Monograph 10. New York: International Universities Press.

Gitelson, M. 1948. Character Synthesis: The Psychotherapeutic Problem of Adolescence. *Amer. J. Orthopsych.* 18:422–431.

———. 1962. The Curative Factors in Psychoanalysis. *Int. J. Psycho-Anal.* 43:194–205.

Glover, E. 1932. A Psycho-Analytic Approach to the Classification of Mental Disorders. In *On the Early Development of the Mind.* New York: International Universities Press, 1956, pp. 161–86.

———. 1943. The Concept of Dissociation. In *On the Early Development of the Mind.* New York: International Universities Press, 1956, pp. 307–23.

———. 1950. Functional Aspects of the Mental Apparatus. In *On the Early Development of the Mind.* New York: International Universities Press, 1956, pp. 364–78.

———. 1968. *The Birth of the Ego.* New York: International Universities Press.

Goldberg, A. 1967. The Psychoanalytic Situation Experienced as a Transitional Object. Presented to the Chicago Institute for Psychoanalysis.

———. 1971. On Waiting. *Int. J. Psycho-Anal.* 52:413–22.

Goldberg, A., and Rubin, B. 1964. Recovery of Patients During Periods of Supposed Neglect. *Brit. J. Med. Psych.* 37:266–272.

———. 1971. A Method of Pacification of the Psychotic Excited State: The Use of the Hospital as a Transitional Object. *Comp. Psych.* 11:450–456.

Greenacre, P. 1967. The Influence of Infantile Trauma on Genetic Patterns. In *Emotional Growth,* New York: International Universities Press, 1971, 1:260–99.

Grinberg, L. 1968. On Acting Out and Its Role in the Psychoanalytic Process. *Int. J. Psycho-Anal.* 49:171–78.

Grinker, R. R., Sr. 1957. On Identification. *Int. J. Psycho-Anal.* 38: 379–90.

———. 1958. A Philosophical Appraisal of Psychoanalysis. In *Science and Psychoanalysis*, Masserman, ed. New York: Grune and Stratton.

———. 1966. "Open-System" Psychiatry. *Amer. J. Psychoanal.* 21: 115–28.

———. 1967. Introduction. In *Toward a Unified Theory of Human Behavior*, R. R. Grinker, ed. 2d ed. New York: Basic Books.

———. 1968. Conceptual Progress in Psychoanalysis. In *Modern Psychoanalysis*, Marmor, ed. New York: Basic Books.

———. 1969. Symbolism and General Systems Theory. In *General Systems Theory and Psychiatry*, Dahl and Rizzo, eds. Boston: Little, Brown and Company.

Hartmann, H. 1939. *Ego Psychology and the Problem of Adaptation.* New York: International Universities Press, 1958.

———. 1950a. Psychoanalysis and Developmental Psychology. In *Essays in Ego Psychology.* New York: International Universities Press, 1964, pp. 99–112.

———. 1950b. Comments on the Psychoanalytic Theory of the Ego. In *Essays in Ego Psychology.* New York: International Universities Press, 1964, pp. 113–41.

———. 1952. The Mutual Influences in the Development of the Ego and the Id. In *Essays in Ego Psychology.* New York: International Universities Press, 1964, pp. 155–81.

———. 1953. Contribution to the Metapsychology of Schizophrenia. In *Essays in Ego Psychology.* New York: International Universities Press, 1964, pp. 182–206.

———. 1956. The Development of the Ego Concept in Freud's Work. In *Essays in Ego Psychology.* New York: International Universities Press, 1964, pp. 268–96.

Hartmann, H., and Kris, E. 1945. The Genetic Approach in Psychoanalysis. In *Papers on Psychoanalytic Psychology.* Psychological Issues Monograph 14. New York: International Universities Press, 1964.

Hartmann, H., Kris, E., and Loewenstein, R. 1946. Comments on the Formation of Psychic Structure. In *Papers on Psychoanalytic Psychology.* Psychological Issues Monograph 14. New York: International Universities Press, 1964, pp. 27–55.

Hartmann, H., and Loewenstein, R. 1962. Notes on the Superego. In *Papers on Psychoanalytic Psychology.* Psychological Issues Monograph 14. New York: International Universities Press, 1964, pp. 144–81.

Jacobson, E. 1964. *The Self and the Object World.* New York: International Universities Press.

Jones, E. 1953–57. *The Life and Work of Sigmund Freud.* 3 volumes. New York: Basic Books.

Katan, M. 1949. Schreber's Delusions of the End of the World. *Psychoanal. Quarterly* 18:60–66.

————. 1950. Schreber's Hallucinations About the Little Men. *Int. J. Psycho-Anal.* 31:32–35.

————. 1953. Schreber's Pre-psychotic Phase. *Int. J. Psycho-Anal.* 34:43–51.

————. 1959. Schreber's Hereafter. *Psychoanal. Study of the Child* 14:314–82.

Kernberg, O. 1970. Factors in the Psychoanalytic Treatment of Narcissistic Personalities. *J. Amer. Psychoanal. Assoc.* 18:51–85.

Khan, M. 1966. Comment on Dr. Naiman's Paper. *Int. J. Psycho-Anal.* 47:293–94.

————. 1969. On the Clinical Provisions of Frustrations, Recognitions and Failures in the Analytic Situation: An Essay on Dr. Michael Balint's Researches on the Theory of Psychoanalytic Technique. *Int. J. Psycho-Anal.* 50:237–48.

Klein, G. 1959. Consciousness in Psychoanalytic Theory: Some Implications for Current Research in Perception. *J. Amer. Psychoanal. Assoc.* 7:5–34.

————. 1968. Psychoanalysis: Ego Psychology. In *International Encyclopedia of the Social Sciences.* New York: The Macmillan Co. & Free Press, pp. 11–31.

Kohut, H. 1960. Beyond the Bounds of the Basic Rule. *J. Amer. Psychoanal. Assoc.* 9:567–86.

————. 1966. Forms and Transformations of Narcissism. *J. Amer. Psychoanal. Assoc.* 14:243–72.

————. 1968. The Psychoanalytic Treatment of Narcissistic Personality Disorders: Outline of a Systematic Approach. *Psychoanal. Study of the Child* 23:86–113.

————. 1971. *The Analysis of the Self.* Psychoanalytic Study of the Child Monograph Series. New York: International Universities Press.

————. 1972. Thoughts on Narcissism and Narcissistic Rage. *The Psychoanal. Study of the Child* 27:360–400.

Kohut, H., and Seitz, P. F. D. 1963. Concepts and Theories of Psychoanalysis. In *Concepts of Personality,* J. Wepman and R. Heine, eds. Chicago: Aldine Publishing Co.

Kuhn, T. 1962. *The Structure of Scientific Revolutions.* Chicago: University of Chicago Press.

Langer, S. 1962. *Philosophy in a New Key.* 2d edition. New York: Mentor Books.

————. 1967. *Mind: An Essay on Human Feeling.* Vol. 1. Baltimore & London: The Johns Hopkins Press.

Lichtenstein, H. 1961. Identity and Sexuality. *J. Amer. Psycho-Anal. Assoc.* 9:179–260.

————. 1964. The Role of Narcissism in the Emergence and Maintenance of Primary Identity. *Int. J. Psycho-Anal.* 45:49–56.

Ludowyk–Gyomroi, E. 1963. The Analysis of a Young Concentration Camp Victim. *Psycho-Anal. Study of the Child* 18:484–510.

Lustman, S. 1967. The Scientific Leadership of Anna Freud. *J. Amer. Psychoanal. Assoc.* 15:810–27.

Mahler, M. 1963. Thoughts about Development and Individuation. *Psychoanal. Study of the Child* 18:307–24.

————. 1965. On the Significance of the Normal Separation-Individuation Phase. In *Drives, Affects, Behavior.* M. Schur, ed. New York: International Universities Press 2:161–69.

————. 1966. Notes on the Development of Basic Moods: The Depressive Affect. In *Psychoanalysis: a General Psychology*, R. Loewenstein, L. Newman, M. Schur, and A. Solnit, eds. New York: International Universities Press, pp. 152–68.

————. 1967. On Human Symbiosis and the Vicissitudes of Individuation. *J. Amer. Psychoanal. Assoc.* 15:740–63.

McLaughlin, F. 1959. Problems of Re-Analysis. Panel Report. *J. Amer. Psychoanal. Assoc.* 7:537–47.

Modell, A. 1968. *Object Love and Reality.* New York: International Universities Press.

Myerson, P. 1966. Comment on Dr. Zetzel's paper. *Int. J. Psycho-Anal.* 47:139–42.

Nagera, H. 1964. On Arrest in Development, Fixation, and Regression. *Psychoanalytic Study of the Child* 19:222–39.

————. 1964. Autoerotism, Autoerotic Activities, and Ego Development. *The Psychoanalytic Study of the Child* 19:240–55.

————. 1966. *Early Childhood Disturbances, the Infantile Neurosis, and the Adulthood Disturbance.* Psychoanalytic Study of the Child Monograph 2. New York: International Universities Press.

Niederland, W. 1951. Three Notes on the Schreber Case. *Psychoanal. Quarterly* 20:579–91.

————. 1959a. Schreber, Father and Son. *Psychoanal. Quarterly* 28:151–60.

————. 1959b. The "Miracled-up" World of Schreber's Childhood. *Psychoanal. Study of the Child* 14:383–413.

————. 1960. Schreber's Father. *J. Amer. Psychoanal. Assoc.* 8:492–99.

————. 1963. Further Data and Memorabilia Pertaining to the Schreber Case. *Int. J. Psycho-Anal.* 44:201–07.

Nunberg, H. 1951. Transference and Reality. *Int. J. Psycho-Anal.* 32:1–9.

Piaget, J. 1971. *Biology and Knowledge.* Chicago: University of Chicago Press.

Piaget, J., and Inhelder, B. 1969. *The Psychology of the Child.* New York: Basic Books.

Rangell, L. 1965. Some Comments on Psychoanalytic Nosology: With Recommendations for Improvement. In *Drives, Affects, and Behavior.* M. Schur, ed. New York: International Universities Press, 2:128–57.

Rapaport, D. 1950. The Theoretical Implications of Diagnostic Testing Procedures. In *The Collected Papers of David Rapaport.* Ed. Merton Gill. New York: Basic Books, 1967, pp. 334–56.

———. 1951a. Paul Schilder's Contribution to the Theory of Thought Processes. *Int. J. Psycho-Anal.* 32:291–301.

———. 1951b. The Conceptual Model of Psychoanalysis. *J. of Personality* 20:56–81.

———. 1967 (1944). The Scientific Methodology of Psycho-Analysis. In *Collected Papers,* pp. 165–220.

———. 1961 (1953). Some Metapsychological Considerations Regarding Activity and Passivity. In *Collected Papers,* pp. 530–68.

———. 1967. (1957). A Theoretical Analysis of the Superego Concept. In *Collected Papers,* pp. 688–709.

———. 1960. *The Structure of Psychoanalytic Theory.* Psychological Issues Monograph 6. New York: International Universities Press.

Rapaport, D., and Gill, M. 1959. The Points of View and Assumptions of Metapsychology. *Int. J. Psycho-Anal.* 40:153–62.

Reich, A. 1960. Pathologic Forms of Self-Esteem Regulation. *The Psychoanalytic Study of the Child* 15:215–32.

Rosenblueth, A. 1971. *Mind and Brain: a Philosophy of Science.* Cambridge: The MIT Press.

Rosenfeld, H. 1969. On the Treatment of Psychotic States by Psychoanalysis: An Historical Approach. *Int. J. Psycho-Anal.* 50:615–32.

Sandler, J., and Joffe, W. 1965. Notes on Obsessional Manifestations in Children. *Psychoanalytic Study of the Child* 20:425–38.

———. 1969. Towards a Basic Psychoanalytic Model. *Int. J. Psycho-Anal.* 50:79–90.

Sandler, J., and Rosenblatt, B. 1962. The Concept of the Representational World. *Psychoanalytic Study of the Child* 17:128–48.

Schlessinger, N., Pollock, G., Sabshin, M., Sadow, L., and Gedo, J. 1966. Psychoanalytic Contributions to Psychotherapy Research. In *Methods of Research in Psychotherapy.* L. Gottschalk, and A. Auerbach, eds. New York: Appleton-Century-Crofts, pp. 334–60.

Schreber, D. 1909. *Memoirs of My Nervous Illness.* I. MacAlpine, and Hunter, eds. London: Wm. Dawson & Sons, 1955.

Schroedinger, E. 1943. *Science and Humanism.* London: Cambridge University Press.

Schur, M. 1966. *The Id and the Regulatory Principles of Mental Functioning.* New York: International Universities Press.

Segal, H. 1969. *Introduction to the Work of Melanie Klein.* New York: Basic Books.

Selesnick, S. 1966. Carl Gustav Jung. In *Psychoanalytic Pioneers.* F. Alexander, B. Eisenstein, and M. Grotjahn, eds. New York: Basic Books, pp. 63–77.

Strachey, J., ed. (1953–   ). *The Standard Edition of the Complete Psychological Works of Sigmund Freud.* 24 volumes. London: The Hogarth Press.

Tabachnick, N. 1967. Self-realization and Self-definition: Two Aspects of Identity Formation. *Int. J. Psycho-Anal.* 48:68–75.

Tolpin, P. 1970. Some Psychic Determinants of Orgastic Dysfunction. *Bull. Phila. Assoc. Psychoanal.* 20:250–54.

Von Bertalanffy, L. 1968. *General Systems Theory.* New York: George Braziller.

Waelder, R. 1936. The Principle of Multiple Function. *Psycho-Anal. Quarterly* 5:45–62.

———. 1962. Psychoanalysis, Scientific Method, and Philosophy. *J. Amer. Psychoanal. Assoc.* 10:617–37.

Weiss, E. 1970. *Sigmund Freud as a Consultant.* New York: Intercontinental Medical Book Corp.

White, R. 1961. The Mother Conflict in Schreber's Psychosis. *Int. J. Psycho-Anal.* 42:55–73.

———. 1963. The Schreber Case Reconsidered in the Light of Psychosocial Concepts. *Int. J. Psycho-Anal.* 44:213–21.

Winnicott, D. 1951. Transitional Objects and Transitional Phenomena. In *Collected Papers.* New York: Basic Books, 1958, pp. 229–42.

———. 1954. Metapsychological and Clinical Aspects of Regression within the Psycho-Analytical Set-up. In *Collected Papers.* New York: Basic Books, pp. 278–94.

———. 1965. A Clinical Study of the Effect of a Failure of Average Expectable Environment on a Child's Mental Functioning. *Int. J. Psycho-Anal.* 46:81–87.

Wolf, E., Gedo, J., and Terman, D. 1972. On the Adolescent Process as a Transformation of the Self. *J. of Youth and Adolesc.* 1:257–72.

Wolf Man, The. 1958. How I Came into Analysis with Freud. *J. Amer. Psychoanal. Assoc.* 6:348–52. Also in Gardiner, M. 1970.

————. 1968. Memoirs of the Wolfman. Part II. *Bulletin Phila. Assoc. Psychoanal.* 18:159–72. Also in Gardiner, M. 1970.

————. 1970. Memoirs of the Wolfman. Part III. *Bulletin Phila. Assoc. Psychoanal.* 20:87–109. Also in Gardiner, M. 1970.

Yorke, C. 1965. Some Metapsychological Aspects of Interpretation. *Brit. J. Med. Psych.* 38:27–42.

Zavitzianos, G. 1967. Problems of Technique in the Analysis of a Juvenile Delinquent. *Int. J. Psycho-Anal.* 48:439–47.

————. 1971. Fetishism and Exhibitionism in the Female and Their Relationship to Psychopathy and Kleptomania. *Int. J. Psycho-Anal.* 52:297–305.

Zetzel, E. 1965. The Theory of Therapy in Relation to a Developmental Model of the Psychic Apparatus. *Int. J. Psycho-Anal.* 46:39–52.

————. 1966. 1965– . Additional Notes upon a Case of Obsessional Neurosis: Freud, 1909. *Int. J. Psycho-Anal.* 47:123–29.

Index

205

DATE DUE

DATE DUE			
MY 10'77			
MY 3 77			
GAYLORD			PRINTED IN U.S.A.